GETTING OUT OF SOUTH CAROLINA'S JUVENILE JUSTICE SYSTEM

Kimberly Nolan

GETTING OUT OF SOUTH CAROLINA'S JUVENILE JUSTICE SYSTEM

Education for Young Incarcerated Offenders

The Carceral Studies Collection

Collection Editors

Ian Cummins & Louis Mendoza

LPp

Thank you to my parents, who have always supported and encouraged me, and my daughter, who inspires me. My partner in crime, Jess, for her willingness to "pull this van over" when things went sideways. Mark and Sue, thank you for reading and rereading. My thanks to Amy, Joe, and Molly, for connecting me along the way as well as to all the amazing educators, who pushed my thinking.

First published in 2024 by Lived Places Publishing

The author and editors have made every effort to ensure the accuracy of information contained in this publication, but assume no responsibility for any errors, inaccuracies, inconsistencies, and omissions. Likewise, every effort has been made to contact copyright holders. If any copyright material has been reproduced unwittingly and without permission the Publisher will gladly receive information enabling them to rectify any error or omission in subsequent editions.

British Library Cataloguing in Publication Data
A CIP record for this book is available from the British Library

ISBN: 9781916704435 (pbk)
ISBN: 9781916704459 (ePDF)
ISBN: 9781916704442 (ePUB)

The right of Kimberly Nolan to be identified as the Author of this work has been asserted by them in accordance with the Copyright, Design and Patents Act 1988.

Cover design by Fiachra McCarthy
Book design by Rachel Trolove of Twin Trail Design
Typeset by Newgen Publishing UK

Lived Places Publishing
Long Island
New York 11789

www.livedplacespublishing.com

Abstract

Children are entering the juvenile justice system at alarming rates. Among the children entering the system, Black males are overrepresented. Education while incarcerated is critical since most children are already behind in basic skills. Children aspire to leave the system with credentials and educational or job opportunities. Many of them are wise enough to know that they need to change their environment to be successful; however, this is a challenge due to their lack of autonomy as minors. Until improvements to the juvenile justice system are made, recidivism rates will continue to be high. This volume explores the experiences of young people who are incarcerated in the South Carolina (SC) juvenile justice system. It highlights the overrepresentation of Black youth in the system. It focuses on the positive role that education can play in supporting young people to rebuild their lives.

Key words

Child abuse and neglect, Child welfare, Food insecurity, Incarceration, Juvenile justice, Mass incarceration, Prison policies School resource officer, Status offense

Contents

Learning objectives

1. Understand how children enter the justice system in South Carolina
2. Understand how the system is set up
3. Understand who works with incarcerated children
4. Understand what it is like to be inside the juvenile justice system
5. Understand how the South Carolina Department of Juvenile Justice can improve

Introduction

This book describes the juvenile justice system in South Carolina from the perspectives of those involved. Information in this book will be helpful to those studying the criminal justice system and adolescents. Stories in the book are compilations of individual experiences and do not reflect a particular person, rather they are the combination of multiple participants. Stories have been created through interviews with judges, sheriffs, probation and parole officers, lawyers, advocates, the formerly incarcerated, and written documents from incarcerated youth. The book is laid out in five chapters:

1. Entering the juvenile system
2. Incarceration in South Carolina: The system
3. Supporting incarcerated juveniles
4. Life inside
5. Recommendations for change

Each chapter follows this format:

> Guiding question(s), Learning outcomes, Content, Summary, Discussion questions, Extension activities, Resources

Chapter 1 provides an overview of the juvenile justice system in South Carolina. Chapters 2 through 4 present more personal and individual stories based on interviews, observations, and research of the South Carolina juvenile justice system. Chapter 5 contains recommendations based on interviews, observations, and best practices.

Meet the author

Kimberly Nolan is a teaching professor in the Graduate School of Education, Northeastern University, specifically, the Doctor of Education program. She has been a full-time faculty member since 2013. Her research interests include school climate, experiential learning, action research, and student-centered schools. Dr Nolan is a leader within Northeastern's Network of Experiential Learning Educators (NExT) in the Graduate School of Education and throughout the university. She is the lead faculty for Northeastern's EdD program in Charlotte, North Carolina.

Dr Nolan has more than 20 years of experience in K-12 education, including experience as a middle school science teacher, K-12 assistant principal, and alternative high school principal. In addition, she has worked in the community college system as a faculty member and administrator.

Author's journey

As a young educator, I worked most passionately with "those" kids. "Those" kids are the ones lingering in the hallway after the bell, smoking on the corner before school, slumped in a chair in front of the principal's office, staying out too late … the trouble-makers. From my very first days running the after-school center in a Boston housing project, I strove to know the kids I worked with, even though I had very little in common with them. As a college senior, I drove into poorer parts of Boston from a wealthy, safe suburb to supervise 12- to 16-year-olds in after-school centers located in basements and long-forgotten lobbies of large, run-down housing buildings. I remember leaving the building in the dark hoping that my car was still there in the parking lot. When the kids got to know me, they would walk me to my car because, in the words of my charges, "Anybody can tell you don't belong here." I found this work rewarding and heartbreaking. Long-time students would disappear, and later I would learn they had been moved into a group home, arrested, shot, or experienced countless other traumatic events.

I moved on to become a middle school science teacher in the Bronx, in New York City. I had enough general science and math credits to get an emergency teaching license despite my total lack of training in education. Thus, I began my career as a teacher. To say the first year was difficult would be a complete understatement. But, by year two, I loved my job, and my assistant principal noted that I had good classroom management because I developed genuine relationships with my students. Difficult kids were frequently moved to my class after getting in trouble elsewhere. After four years of teaching, I had a master's degree in education and a true license. I wanted more; I wanted to be an administrator. I went on to obtain a master's in educational leadership and secured a job as dean of students at a middle school in rural New England. While working as an administrator, I earned my doctorate in education leadership and policy. I became an assistant principal at the middle school and later a principal at an alternative high school.

All the while, children with behavior issues became "my" kids. Time and time again, I found that "my" kids were not well understood. Their basic needs got in the way of education and classroom structure. Sleeping at their desk was not a sign of disrespect; it was necessary because they had been up all night with the police in their building for a drug raid. They were angry that they had to fight so hard just to get by. It made no sense to them that they had to sit still and take notes on a lecture that did not relate to them. They were hungry, tired, not sure what they would go home to, unsure as to where they would spend the night, so why did grammar matter? These students spent more time in my office, or the in-school suspension room attached to my office, than they did in class. They needed a safe space with adults they trusted. As the students got older, they spent less time in school and more time suspended or skipping class. Eventually, far too many of them vanished into the world of prison.

Do not mistake my empathy and love of at-risk kids with a tolerance for bad behavior. I expect and, most of the time, have earned superior behavior from children—it is earned not given. Early in my career in NYC, I took a weeklong trip to upstate NY to an environmental center with 100 kids and 3 teachers. I think the only reason my assistant principal agreed to the trip was because he didn't think I could raise the money or get the extra chaperones; he was clear that schools like ours did not do overnight field trips with these kids. There were no behavioral incidents other than a little homesickness and general joy. Thank you, Dad, for chaperoning and braving the "wilderness" with me and my crazy idea.

This story of high expectations coupled with mutual respect and providing kids with the opportunity to be successful has been the backdrop of my educational philosophy. Some wonder why don't I go back to a middle school or high school setting if I care so much? The sad truth is that educators working with poorer districts get paid the least and receive the least support. The burnout rate is high, and the hours are never-ending. As a mother, I chose a job that was more flexible, more stable, and left me emotionally able to be present at home. As an educator, I volunteer on the boards of nonprofits that work with "those" kids. Currently, I volunteer at a local juvenile prison with a group that works with incarcerated children on communication skills, and I am a guardian ad litem. This work with incarcerated youth has led me back to my passion for giving voice to and advocating for children in need. I am hoping this book sheds light on the real struggles and successes, however few, of the system that takes "my" kids.

This book explores the root causes of juvenile incarceration and issues within the juvenile system. I am not in any way suggesting that bad behavior should be tolerated, rather that the system should truly be restorative and aimed at improving lives. I have made a conscious choice to refer to the juvenile inmates and juveniles associated with the justice system as "children" because I strongly believe they are still children, both biologically and mentally.

Background

South Carolina, located in the southeastern part of the United States, had a population of 5.08 million in 2021 (Census

Data USA). The median household income was $58,234, and 14.5% of the population lived below the poverty line. This Republican state was 63% White and 26% Black, according to Census Data USA. The education level of the population of the state was 3.4% GED or equivalent, 20.5% high school diploma, 14% bachelor's degree, 5.9% master's degree, and 0.88% doctorate.

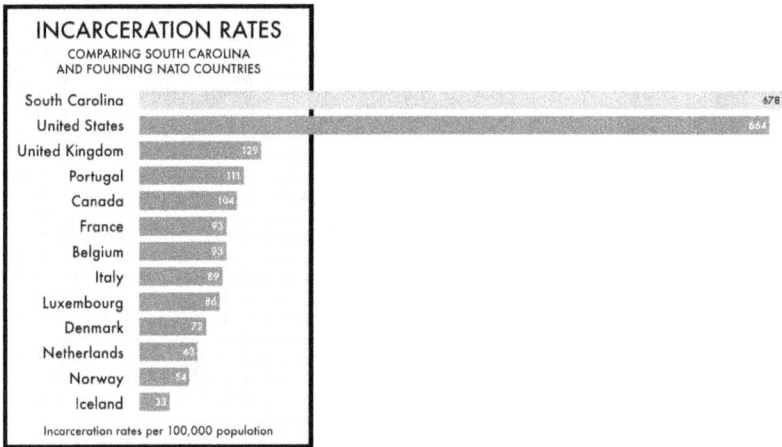

INCARCERATION RATES
COMPARING SOUTH CAROLINA
AND FOUNDING NATO COUNTRIES

Country	Rate
South Carolina	678
United States	664
United Kingdom	129
Portugal	111
Canada	104
France	93
Belgium	93
Italy	89
Luxembourg	86
Denmark	72
Netherlands	63
Norway	54
Iceland	33

Incarceration rates per 100,000 population

Source: https://www.prisonpolicy.org/global/2021.html

Source: https://www.prisonpolicy.org/global/2021.html
Note: Up-to-date juvenile data is difficult to locate since reporting on minors is heavily regulated and different states use different definitions

As seen in the chart, the overall incarceration rate (adults and juveniles) in the United States was 664 per 100,000 people in 2021, and South Carolina's rate was even higher at 678.

Comparing South Carolina's resident and incarcerated populations

Percentage of state residents, by race or ethnicity, compared to the percentage of people in the state's prisons in 2021 and in local jails in 2019, by race or ethnicity. Compared to the total state population, Black people are overrepresented in the incarcerated population, while white people are underrepresented.

Residents	Prisons	Jails	Residents	Prisons	Jails	Residents	Prisons	Jails	Residents	Prisons	Jails	Residents	Prisons	Jails
63%	37%	49%	26%	59%	48%	6%	3%	3%	0.2%	0.2%	0.1%	2%	0.1%	0.1%
WHITE non-Hispanic			BLACK non-Hispanic			HISPANIC			AMER. INDIAN OR ALASKA NATIVE non-Hispanic			ASIAN non-Hispanic		

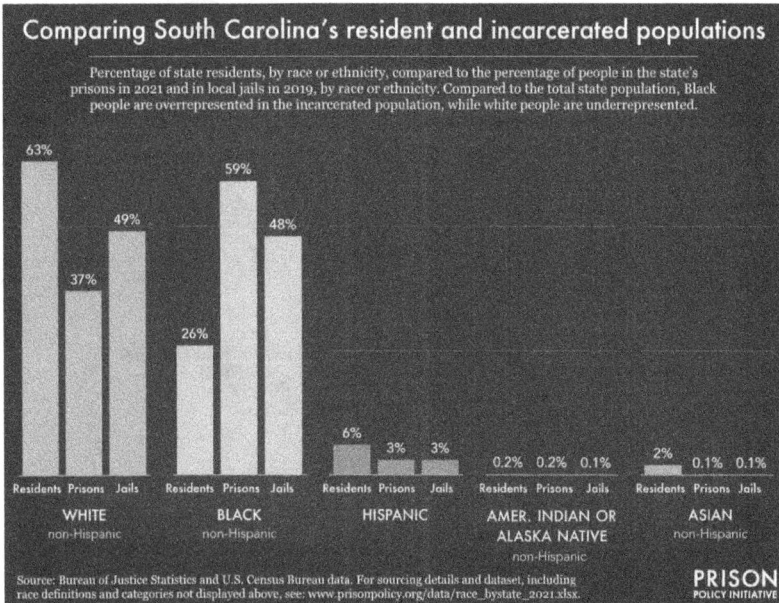

Source: Bureau of Justice Statistics and U.S. Census Bureau data. For sourcing details and dataset, including race definitions and categories not displayed above, see: www.prisonpolicy.org/data/race_bystate_2021.xlsx.

PRISON POLICY INITIATIVE

Source: Bureau of Justice Statistics and U.S. Census Bureau data. For sourcing details and dataset, including race definitions and categories not displayed above, see www.prisonpolicy.org/data/race_bystate_2021.xlsx.

As seen above, the percentage of Black South Carolinians in prison was disproportionately higher than that of the general population in 2021. Black citizens of South Carolina were incarcerated at a rate 3.8 times higher than White citizens (Prison Policy; Widra and Herring, 2021). South Carolina ranked #34 among U.S. states for White incarceration rates and #44 for Black incarceration rates.

Looking at the juvenile population in South Carolina, the incarceration rate was 84 per 100,000 persons (ranking #33 among all states) compared to the U.S. average of 114 per 100,000. This average was skewed by very high incarceration rates in states such as Alaska, which had 330 per 100,000. Current juvenile statistics are difficult to obtain since states do not have the same juvenile laws and systems. Each state treats juveniles slightly differently.

Youth

State	Rate
Alaska	330
West Virginia	291
District of Columbia	262
Wyoming	239
South Dakota	180
Nevada	174
Idaho	164
Oregon	164
Alabama	161
Indiana	161
Minnesota	161
Michigan	157
Ohio	148
Arkansas	146
Nebraska	145
Louisiana	143
South Carolina	141
Delaware	139
Iowa	133
Montana	133
Colorado	130
Kentucky	130
Pennsylvania	129
Texas	126
New Mexico	122
USA	114
Rhode Island	114
Kansas	113
Georgia	110
Virginia	109
Missouri	108
Florida	104
North Dakota	104
California	102
Washington	94
North Carolina	93
Wisconsin	93
Maryland	82
Arizona	80
Oklahoma	80
Illinois	64
Mississippi	61
New Jersey	58
Utah	58
New York	54
Maine	51
Tennessee	50
Hawaii	49
Massachusetts	46
Vermont	33
Connecticut	27
New Hampshire	20

Most states' juvenile courts have jurisdiction over people under age 18. Georgia, Texas, and Wisconsin exclude 17-year olds from their juvenile courts.

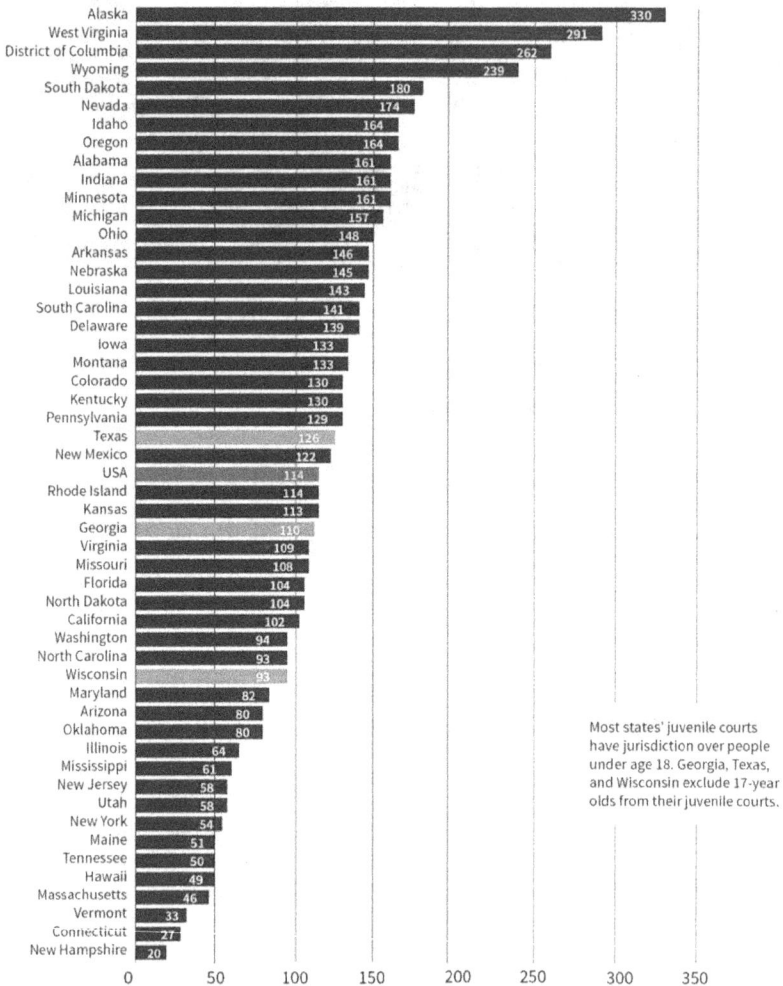

Source: The Sentencing Project (2023).

Note: Youth Placement rate by state (2019). Placement rate per 100,000 juveniles.

In South Carolina, a juvenile is someone who is age 18 or younger. Someone 18 years or younger can be "waived up" to adult court based on the waiver chart § 63-19-1210. The following is a summary of the waivers:

A family court judge has the authority to waive a child who is:

- any age and charged with murder. *State v. Corey D.*, 529 S.E.2d 20 (S.C. 2000); *State v. Lamb*, 649 S.E.2d 486 (S.C. 2007).
- 17 and charged with a misdemeanor, a Class E or F felony, or a felony that would carry a maximum term of imprisonment of ten years or less for an adult, after a full investigation. § 63-19-1210(4).
- 14, 15, or 16 years of age and charged with an offense that would be a Class A, B, C, or D felony or a felony that provides for a maximum term of imprisonment of 15 years or more for an adult, after full investigation and a hearing. § 63-19-1210(5).
- 14 years or older and charged with carrying a weapon on school property, unlawful carrying of a handgun, or unlawful distribution of drugs within a half-mile of a school, after a full investigation and a hearing. § 63-19-1210(9).
- A child under 14 years is prohibited under § 16-3-659 from being transferred to general sessions court on a criminal sexual conduct charge. *Slocumb v. State*, 522 S.E.2d 809 (S.C. 1999).

The eight "Kent Factors" are used to determine whether a waiver will be granted. The court must consider eight factors enumerated in *Kent v. United States*, 383 U.S. 541 (1966), before granting a motion to transfer jurisdiction, and the serious nature of the offense is a major factor in the transfer decision, see *State v. Pittman*, 647 S.E.2d 144 (S.C. 2007) and *State v. Corey D.*,529 S.E.2d 20, 26 (S.C. 2000). The eight factors of *Kent* are as follows:

1. Seriousness of alleged offense and whether a waiver is necessary to protect the public;
2. Whether the alleged offense was committed in an aggressive, violent, premeditated, or willful manner;
3. Whether the alleged offense was against persons or property, greater weight was being given to offenses against persons especially if an injury resulted;
4. Whether there is sufficient evidence for a grand jury to return an indictment;
5. Whether there are adult co-defendants that make it more desirable to present the entire case in one court;
6. Child's level of sophistication and maturity;
7. Child's prior criminal record; and
8. Prospects for adequate protection of the public and likelihood of reasonable rehabilitation of child using services currently available to the court.

The decision to "waive" children up to adult court strips some of the protections from the family court such as a focus on restorative justice. This puts children in a position to face harsher and more punitive punishments. When cases are moved to adult court, the reformative values of family court are lost.

The current system of juvenile justice in South Carolina

The South Carolina Department of Juvenile Justice (SCDJJ) is responsible for providing custodial care and rehabilitation for the state's children who are incarcerated, on probation or parole, or in community placement for a criminal or status offense. DJJ also provides a variety of prevention and intervention programs for at-risk youth. SCDJJ defines its role as follows:

Mission: impact and transform young lives, strengthen families, and support safer communities through targeted prevention and rehabilitation.

Vision: youth discover their strengths and abilities and become productive and successful citizens contributing to a safer South Carolina.

DJJ has many facilities throughout the state with different pur poses. The Juvenile Detention Center is a pretrial detention facility to hold juveniles pending trial. Evaluation centers hold juveniles for court-ordered evaluations after a child has been adjudicated. The Broad River Road Complex (BRRC) is for long-term commitment to serve a longer determinate or indeterminate sentence. In addition, there are alternative placements throughout the state, although it is important to note that fewer than 38% of all juveniles needing placement can be accommodated at these alternative placements. There are 218 available beds for males and only 20 beds for females in alternative placements in the entire state. The daily average population of DJJ beds is 621 (SCDJJ *Data Resource Guide* 2020–2021, p. 2). According to the 2020–2021 *Data Resource Guide*, 127 alternative beds (undefined by DJJ) are being used, serving 20% of the juvenile population in DJJ.

Juvenile Detention Center

DJJ's Juvenile Detention Center is a centralized pretrial detention facility serving juveniles from most of South Carolina's 46 counties. (Several counties, including Richland and Charleston, operate their short-term detention facilities.) The Detention Center is a secure, short-term facility providing custodial care and acute treatment to male and female juveniles ages 11 to 19 who are detained by law enforcement agencies for alleged offenses committed prior to their eighteenth birthday, according to the DJJ website. A child may be in a detention center for a day, while others can be held for years, depending on the charges and how backed up the courts are. It is important to note that children cannot bond out or post bail while waiting for court like adults can. Youth ordered to cooperate with a psychiatric and educational evaluation may also be ordered by the family courts to be detained before disposition. Youth awaiting trial on serious and violent charges reside at DJJ's Juvenile Detention Center to ensure public safety and their immediate availability for court proceedings.

Evaluation centers

In the current configuration of DJJ, there are three regional evaluation centers: Coastal, Midlands, and Upstate. Each of the agency's evaluation centers provides court-ordered evaluations for adjudicated youth (those found guilty) prior to the final disposition of their cases. The evaluation centers provide comprehensive psychological, social, and educational assessments to guide the court's disposition of cases. Evaluation centers also house youth in admissions status, meaning youth who are court-ordered to be committed to DJJ for a determinate or indeterminate sentence. Youth in admissions status are screened by a multidisciplinary team to determine an appropriate treatment and housing assignment. By law, the length of stay for youth undergoing a secure evaluation cannot exceed 45 days (see DJJ website).

Broad River Road Complex (BRRC)

The Broad River Road Complex in Columbia is the agency's long-term commitment facility. The more than 200-acre complex offers programs for boys and girls of different backgrounds and needs, including programs for youth with behavioral issues and special needs.

BRRC is also the home base to DJJ's fully accredited school district, which provides continued education for youth, preparing students for postsecondary education and beyond. The Empowerment & Enrichment Academy of South Carolina (formerly Birchwood School) is where boys and girls attend middle and high school and can also earn their GEDs. This campus also includes DJJ's Junior Reserve Officer Training Corps (JROTC) program, a cooperative effort between DJJ's school district and the U.S. army, and various enriching vocational programs.

In addition to school and vocational options, BRRC offers social work and psychology services, treatment planning, psychiatry services, a full infirmary for health care needs, gyms, open fields, a game room incentive building, recreation, and various types of rehabilitative programs and work programs.

Alternative placement facilities
Low country

Beaufort Marine Institute, Beaufort County, Males, 30 beds

Midlands

Camp Aspen, Richland County, Males, 30 beds
Camp White Pines, Union County, Males, 40 beds
Gateways, Richland County, Males, 12 beds

Generations, Richland Country, Males, 26 beds (this is not listed on the website but was provided by DJJ in a personal communication, 2024)

Pee Dee

Camp Bennettsville, Marlboro County, Males, 20 beds
Camp Sand Hills, Chesterfield County, Males, 30 beds
Georgetown Marine Institute, Georgetown County, Males, 30 beds

Upstate

Generations Bridges, Greenville County, Males, 26 beds
Piedmont Wilderness Institute, Laurens County, Females, 20 beds

According to the 2019 DJJ report card, 11,849 cases were referred to South Carolina DJJ. The number one charge referred to was third-degree assault and battery followed by marijuana possession, truancy, runaway, and contempt of court. Below is a table showing the four stages of system involvement. Referrals are youth who enter the DJJ system when they are taken into custody by law enforcement or when they are charged by a solicitor or school. Detained youth are those facing charges or those being held at a facility being formally referred. Of those cases referred, some youth are detained pending court. The average detainment is 22 days; the longest (sent to court in 2020) was 879 days (approximately 2.5 years). Evaluations happen at one of the three evaluation centers or in the community. Youth are not supposed to be held in evaluation centers for more than 45 days before trial. Commitments are those who have gone to court and received sentences.

2019/2020

	Referred to DJJ	**Detained**	**Evaluation**	**Commitment**
Total	1107	136	71	46
Sex				
Male	70%	79%	81%	84%
	(n=775)	(n=107)	(n=58)	(n=39)
Female	30%	21%	19%	16%
	(n=332)	(n=29)	(n=13)	(n=7)
Race				
Black	55%	72%	61%	65%
	(n=609)	(n=98)	(n=44)	(n=30)
White	39%	21%	33%	28%
	(n=432)	(n=29)	(n=23)	(n=13)

	Referred to DJJ	Detained	Evaluation	Commitment
Other	6% (n=66)	7% (n=9)	6% (n=4)	7% (n=3)
Age				
13 and under	16% (n=177)	7% (n=9)	11% (n=9)	22% (n=9)
14–16	57% (n=631)	64% (n=88)	68% (n=48)	56% (n=25)
17+	26% (n=288)	29% (n=39)	19% (n=14)	29% (n=12)

Note: Numbers do not add up to 100%. This is the data published by SCDJJ.

	Referred to DJJ	Detained	Evaluation	Commitment
Most Common Offenses	Assault 3rd Degree	Assault 3rd Degree	Contempt of Court	Probation Violation Felony
	Marijuana Possession	Weapon Carrying Pistol	Assault 3rd Degree	Contempt of Court
	Truancy		Weapon	Probation Violation
	Runaway	Runaway	Assault 2nd Degree	Misdemeanors
	Contempt	Armed Robbery	Carrying Pistol	Probation Violation Felony
				Weapons

Definition of offenses

Assault 3rd Degree—misdemeanor offense that involves injuring or attempting to injure another person without legal justification.

Truancy—missing too many days of school that are not approved.

Runaway—a person under 18 years of age who has willfully left home without the permission of parent(s) and/or legal guardian.

Contempt of Court—willful disobedience of a court's lawful process, order, directive, or instruction.

Weapon—possession of a firearm or visible display of what appears to be a firearm or visible display of a knife during the commission of a violent crime.

Carrying a Pistol—carrying a handgun whether concealed or not, except when authorized by law.

Armed Robbery—a felony that involves committing robbery while armed with a deadly weapon or while pretending to be armed with a deadly weapon.

Assault 2nd Degree—injuring or threatening another person without legal reason, causing "moderate bodily harm".

Possession of Marijuana—28 grams (1 ounce) or less.

Probation Violation Felony/Misdemeanor—violation of terms of probation; the seriousness and conditions of probation determine felony or misdemeanor.

Felonies—are considered more serious than misdemeanors and carry potential prison time. A felony is defined under federal law as any crime whose punishment exceeds one year in prison. However, some states, like South Carolina, have their own criminal laws and punishments that stray from federal definitions. The conviction for a second or subsequent offense is a felony in South Carolina.

Status Offenses—only minors can be charged with these:

Truancy—violation of a compulsory school attendance law.

Running away—leaving the custody and home of parents or guardians without permission and failing to return within a reasonable length of time.

Incorrigibility—A child is considered incorrigible when the child repeatedly or habitually disobeys the direction of the child's lawful parents, guardians, or legal custodians.

Per the Office of Juvenile Justice and Delinquency Prevention (OJJDP) with the U.S. Department of Justice, states should not detain children on status offenses. South Carolina currently incarcerates children on status offenses. Advocacy groups such as the Children's Law Center are working to change detention for status offenses.

Questions to consider

What disparities do you notice in the data displayed in terms of race, gender, and age? Why are 70% of referrals males and 84% of commitment males? What would explain why 55% of referrals are for Black children and 65% of commitments are for Black children?

National recidivism

Nationwide, there is no definition or statistics for juvenile recidivism, according to OJJDP. Snyder and Sickmund (2006) showed a 55% rearrest rate and a 24% return to confinement for juveniles within one year of release. The national average for adult recidivism is 37.1% (wisevoter.com).

Recidivism rates, with recidivism defined by SCDJJ as youth who are adjudicated for a new offense within one year of completing arbitration, probation, or commitment (SCDJJ *Data Resource Guide* 2022–2023), were 35.6% from 2019 to 2022 per DOJ data. Hernandez (2023) reported that South Carolina had an adult recidivism rate of 21%, the lowest in the country. Since there is no standard national definition for recidivism, this rate needs to be further explored.

Recidivism rate for those initially arrested before age 17

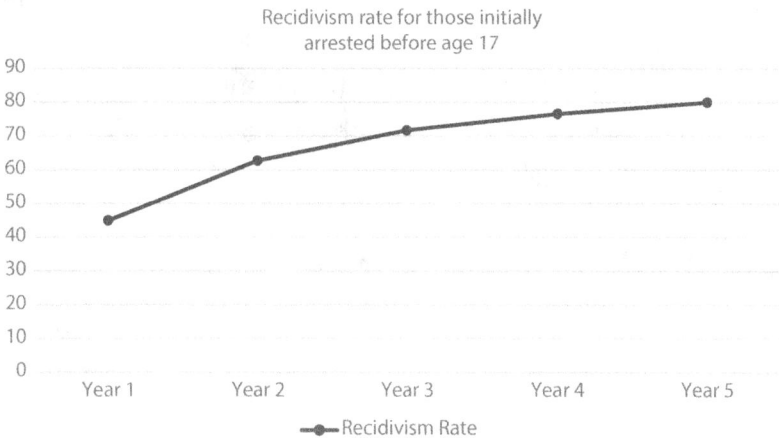

—●—Recidivism Rate

As seen above, the five-year recidivism rate can look bleak for youth. In year 1, the recidivism rate is 44.9% and by year 5, it is 80%.

Summary

In this chapter, the data for incarceration was presented. The United States incarcerates more individuals than any other developed nation. In future chapters, the book will discuss what it is like in DSS custody, how children get out of DJJ custody, and what comes next. In Chapter 1, there will be a discussion of how children enter the justice system.

Discussion questions

1. What do you already know about the juvenile justice system?
2. What is your image of a juvenile in the justice system? Has your image changed based on the data provided?
3. What charges were you expecting juveniles to be arrested for? Which of the most common charges was surprising? Why?
4. Children as young as 11 are in the juvenile justice system. Is this surprising? What do you think about this based on 11-year-olds you know?

Extension activities

1. Opinion/Research—What does juvenile incarceration say about society? How do other countries handle youth who commit crimes?
2. Interview—Interview someone involved in the juvenile justice system. What is their role? How would they improve the juvenile justice system? What obstacles stand in the way of improvement?
3. Research—Look at your home state's juvenile justice system. What is the rate of incarceration for youth? What are the alternatives in your state? What do you notice when you look at the data?

Resources

Advancement Project. (2013, July 3). *The school to prison pipeline.* [Video] YouTube. Available at: https://www.youtube.com/watch?v=YnGctoUq-fA.

The Annie E. Casey Foundation. (2021). *Change indicator: Youth residing in juvenile detention, correctional and/or residential facilities in United States.* [Online] Kids Count Data Center. Available at: https://datacenter.aecf.org/data/tables/42-youth-residing-in-juvenile-detention-correctional-and-or-residential-facilit ies?loc=1&loct=2&msclkid=ecde2e556b561f1646784b591923a 7b5&utm_source=bing&utm_medium=cpc&utm_campaign= Juvenile%20Detention%20-%20Topics&utm_term=what%20 is%20juvenile%20detention&utm_content=What%20is%20J uvenile%20Detention#detailed/2/2-52/false/871,573,36,867,13 3,18,17,14,12,10/any/319,17599.

Nelson, L. and Lind, D. (2015, October 27). *The school-to-prison pipeline, explained.* [Online] Vox. Available at: https://www.vox.com/2015/2/24/8101289/school-discipline-race#Black%20S tudents%20Are%20More%20Likely%20to%20Be%20Disciplined.

South Carolina Department of Juvenile Justice. *Publications and documents.* Available at: https://djj.sc.gov/.

1
Entering the juvenile system

Guiding Question: How do children enter the juvenile justice system?

Learning outcomes

- Understand how children enter the justice system.
- Understand who enters the system.
- Understand the backstory of children entering the system.

National DJJ background

How do kids go from living a regular life as a teenager to entering the justice system? It can happen in three basic ways: children are arrested in the community for a crime, children are referred to the system for a crime, or police are called to the home by parents. Once a child enters the system, they may be detained pending trial or left in the community until trial. Nationally, juvenile justice spans the spectrum from very punitive to restorative. As a country, the United States allows each state to determine independently how to respond to juveniles and to criminal infractions as a whole. As a result, what happens to an offender is very dependent on their age and the state in which they offend. Each state sets the age for treating people as juveniles versus adults, and each state determines where different people are incarcerated. Overall, the United States has a juvenile incarceration rate of three times that of any other developed nation (Widra and Herring, 2021). This chapter will describe the national picture of juvenile justice and dive deeper into four common scenarios of children in the South Carolina juvenile justice system. Each scenario is followed by background information from the literature to situate the reader's understanding of the issues on a national and state level.

Biology tells us that adolescents are not developmentally prepared to make adult decisions, yet these juveniles are being incarcerated, in many cases as adults (Cavanagh, 2022). It is developmentally appropriate for youth to engage in risky behaviors. Research shows that this phenomenon has an important developmental function: these early risk-taking experiences prepare us for adulthood, leading us to be more willing to take on important new challenges later in life, such as starting a job or leaving home (Human Impact Partners, 2017). Charging youth as adults directly ignores this science of adolescent development. Children undergo two transitions when they are incarcerated as adults: a developmental transition from child to adult and an institutional transition from living in the community to being incarcerated, according to Altschuler and Brash (2004). Juveniles need help to work through both transitions. If there is hope for success, this is the time for intervention. Historically, it has been proven that education and skills training of incarcerated individuals reduces recidivism rates by 13% and is cost effective. Every dollar spent on correctional education saves $5 in three-year reincarceration costs, according to the RAND Corporation's 2014 annual report.

A student's time incarcerated is a time to increase their learning and skill development to get them closer to grade level or to the level of entering a career. The youth in the juvenile justice system face many barriers to completing their education while they are held in facilities (and once they are released). Unfortunately, 66% of youth do not return to school after being released from secure custody (Federal Interagency Reentry Council, 2012). We need more proactive programming to prepare our youth to reenter society and meet or exceed community expectations. As RAND (2015) suggests, we cannot afford not to.

What happens to juveniles when they enter the juvenile prison system? In most cases, juveniles receive little education and/or skills training while incarcerated, if any. Their academic and social skills decrease after they are held for committing an offense, putting them at a further disadvantage. Aizer and Doyle (2015) suggest that juvenile incarceration results in significantly lower high school completion rates and higher adult incarceration rates. This should signal that something needs to be done to route juveniles away from the system of incarceration, and, when that is not possible, more resources need to be allocated to those incarcerated.

In South Carolina, the national concerns of high juvenile incarceration, high recidivism, and low educational skills are also apparent. Children held in these state facilities are treated as inmates, much as their adult counterparts are treated, despite their age and developmental stage. Many lawsuits have been filed against the SCDJJ, most recently a civil suit from the ACLU of South Carolina. According to a lawsuit filed in April 2022 in the U.S. District Court, District of South Carolina, children held in SCDJJ facilities are routinely subjected to violence, months-long isolation in solitary confinement, and a lack of meaningful educational or mental health services. These inmates, students, are frequently denied adequate schooling due to overcrowding, lack of staff, and safety issues. When youth are incarcerated, they need intense work in academic and social skills to enable them to return to and succeed in a setting where they were previously unsuccessful. Students entering the system are usually already behind and frequently considered to be of low intelligence and have poor academic achievement (Altschuler and Brash, 2004). They need more help than they had before they were incarcerated, rather than less.

John's story

John, a 15-year-old White male, is repeatedly cited and subsequently arrested for selling marijuana near his house. John lives in a neighborhood of low-income houses and families struggling to get by. He is one of many teens who are out late at night and have inconsistent attendance at school. During his arrest, John is found to have a knife in his possession. Given the drug charge, weapon, and his history with police, John is sent to the evaluation center pending sentencing or release. He is transported in a police car in handcuffs to the facility where he is processed in. When he is called to court 20 days later, he explains that he has five siblings and his mom works as many jobs as she can get. John's mother is having to choose between paying rent and putting food on the table. Despite her work at a fast-food restaurant and other odd jobs, she is unable to provide the necessities for her children. As the oldest, John needs to help feed and meet the basic needs of his siblings. School and other activities are secondary. John's revelation in court gets some recommendations for food banks and he is sent home on probation, time served.

Background on food insecurity

The USDA defines food insecurity as "limited or uncertain access to adequate food" (USDA, 2023). The two parts of the definition are important to separate out: one is quantity, and the other is quality. Unlimited access to Cheetos is not food security. Without proper nutrition, teens are jeopardizing their physical development (malnutrition, diabetes, obesity, lowered immunity, cardiac disease), education (missed school, delayed brain development, behavior that results in being removed from class), and mental health (anxiety, depression, stress, substance abuse, behavior disorders). Food insecurity does not receive as much attention as generalized poverty but takes a huge toll on teenagers.

Food insecurity leads to physical developmental issues including diabetes, obesity, heart disease, and many others. Obesity is linked to diabetes, heart disease, stroke, and cancer. The physical impact of food insecurity then leads to negative educational results. Young brains are more vulnerable to the impact of nutrient deficiency than those of adults. According to the *Journal of Pediatrics* (Cusick and Georgieff, 2016), brain development supported by good nutrition influences positive impulse control, attention, mental health, and social-emotional skills. The cycle starting with poor nutrition from food insecurity can lead to illness and lack of development physically, mentally, and educationally and ends in illness and other negative results (Castle, 2019).

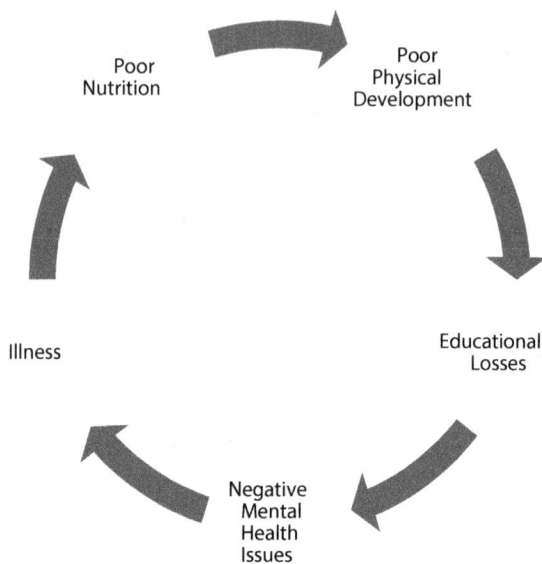

Food insecurity is not just a lack of food, but a lack of safe, nutritious food. This means food that is not spoiled or out of date, food that is healthy, not just cheap junk food. For example, a fast-food hamburger is cheaper than a salad with grilled chicken. The reliance on cheap, poor-quality food is part of the issue (USDA, 2023).

According to the Feeding America report, in 2016, 6.8 million Americans between the ages of 10 and 17 were food insecure, meaning they did not have enough to eat and the threat of running out of food at any time was a reality (Pokin, Scott and Galvez, 2016). According to Coleman-Jenson et al. (2018), approximately 16% of U.S. households are food insecure with limited or uncertain access to safe, nutritious food.

Prevalence of food insecurity, average 2019–21

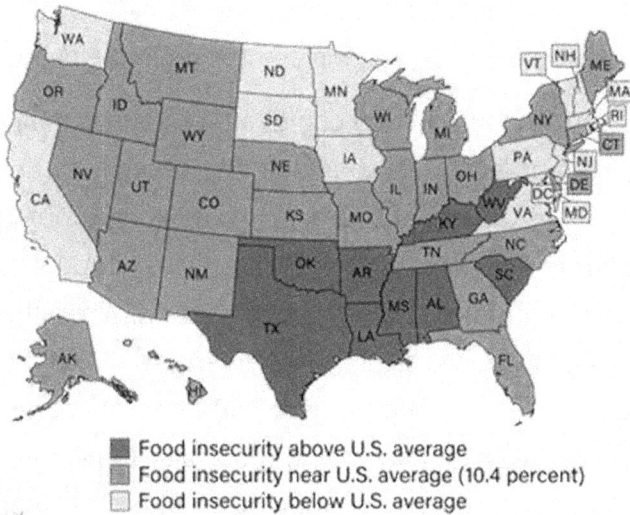

■ Food insecurity above U.S. average
▨ Food insecurity near U.S. average (10.4 percent)
□ Food insecurity below U.S. average

Source: USDA, Economic Research Service using data from U.S. Department of Commerce, Bureau of the Census, 2019, 2020, and 2021 Current Population Survey Food Security Supplements.

Source: USDA, Economic Research Service using data from U.S. Department of Commerce, Bureau of the Census, 2019, 2020, and 2021 Current Population Survey Food Security Supplements.

Food insecurity and poverty significantly impact how teens behave. This is a general discussion of food insecurity and teens (not John's story specifically).

> Food-insecure teens who don't get enough to eat sometimes resort to extreme measures to cope with hunger—from saving school lunches for the weekend or going hungry so younger siblings can eat to stealing or trading sex for money to buy food. (Popkin, Scott and Galvez, 2016, p. 1)

Not all food-insecure teens resort to risky behavior, but teens living with food insecurity and taking on the role of trying to feed younger siblings frequently do resort to criminal activity.

The move to criminal activity comes after teens fail to find legitimate jobs—or legitimate jobs that pay enough to help their families. Teens describe augmenting their minimum-paying jobs starting with smaller crimes such as going through a store's self-checkout and not scanning all their items. When this is not enough, teens resort to stealing larger items to sell on the street. Many teens take up selling drugs to make ends meet. Teens frequently balance school, work, and drug sales to help feed their families. Many teens don't give up school because that could get them in trouble with the police, but, ironically, they are selling drugs at school. Research put out by the Partnership to End Addiction frequently recognizes that 60% of high school students can get drugs at school, and marijuana is the most commonly sold drug in U.S. high schools (Salmassi, 2012).

Girls are more likely than boys to resort to selling themselves to earn money for their families. Interviews with teen girls show that they do not consider themselves to be prostitutes; rather, they are trading: "if I had sex with you, you have to buy me dinner tonight … that's better than taking money because if they take money, they will be labeled a prostitute" (Popkin, Scott and Galvez, 2016, p. 16). Girls actively seek older men who seem to have money to "date" so they can get things such as food, money, jewelry, and so on. Boys were more likely to steal and sell drugs and exchange sex for resources.

Deputy Fields

From school to the justice system in an hour: a student at Spring Valley High School was asked by a teacher to put her phone away, and she refused. A school administrator asked her to leave the classroom, and she refused. The school resource officer (SRO) was called. Then, in a now-infamous 15-second video taken by other students in the classroom and posted on social media, anyone can see the student get arrested. Heavy.com news outlet and many others reported on the video that shows a White officer grabbing the Black student by the arm as she sits at her desk. The officer asks her to leave the classroom with him, and when she refuses, he pulls on her arm, moving the desk and the girl, and then grabs hold of her shoulder and neck area. As she falls backward, she throws her arm up and hits the officer in the jaw. He turns over the desk, throwing it and the girl, he then drags her toward the door, pulling the desk along with her. Once she is out of the chair, he jumps on top of her to handcuff her. The girl's lawyer, Todd Rutherford, said she was injured. She has a cast on her arm, and she suffered back and neck injuries, along with a rug burn to her face. According to the attorney, the unnamed girl recently entered foster care after the death of her mother. The 16-year-old student was arrested for disturbing the peace.

Richland County Sheriff, Leon Lott, confirmed in multiple news outlets that charges were not dropped even though he announced that Deputy Fields was put on suspension and later let go. Another student who tried to intervene on the girl's behalf was also arrested for disturbing the peace.

Another student identified as Tony Robinson told WLTX-TV, "I've never seen anything so nasty looking, so sick to the point that other students are turning away." Robinson described the students as "scared for their lives" and added, "That's supposed to be someone that's going to protect us. Not somebody to be scared of."

In addition, Niya Kenny, another student, got involved when she tried to defend the unnamed girl. This resulted in Kenny being charged with disturbing the school and arrested as well. Kenny told WLTX-TV that Fields was yelling at her when she spoke up to defend her classmate (Cleary, 2021). I was praying out loud for the girl", Kenny told the news station. "I just couldn't believe this was happening." Kenny, 18, was charged with disturbing the school, a misdemeanor, and released on $1,000 bond (Cleary, 2021).

This incident was turned into a larger documentary titled *On These Grounds* (Simonpillai, 2021) . In the documentary, Vivian Anderson, an advocate for Black girls, led the charge to raise awareness of police impact in schools and created a group called Every Black Girl. She has worked to empower Black girls to speak up and fight against injustice.

Those in favor of police in schools cite the counternarrative *Why Meadow Died*. Fields attended a session with one of the authors of this book, Max Eden. Fields expressed his opinion that the school-to-prison pipeline was a myth. Eden describes that taking away the power of teachers and SROs is making schools more dangerous in his book. Fields discussed his belief in stopping bad behavior in schools throughout the documentary *On These Grounds*. Many believe that there is a direct line between being in trouble in school and winding up in prison as an adult. *On These Grounds* portrays the relationship between race and school discipline.

Background on SROs

Richland County has the largest school resource officer (SRO) program in South Carolina SROs are sworn law enforcement officers assigned to a school. Some officers work full-time in one school, while others split their time between school and other duties. They work with school administrators to ensure school safety. It is critical that SROs are trained in child development and understand that children are not tiny adults; rather, they have not fully developed cognitively. Hopefully, SROs are creating relationships with students so they can mentor and support children.

However, placing SROs in schools remains controversial. In 2020, there were an estimated 20,000 SROs in schools (Justice Policy Institute, 2020). Critics, such as the Center for Public Justice, claim that law enforcement in schools is perpetuating the school-to-prison pipeline by making it more likely that children of color are arrested because of police proximity to students. Discipline that should be managed by school officials has become an arrestable offense, and this creates a hostile environment for already at-risk youth. Minor school infractions are introducing students to the justice system, which could stay with them for a lifetime. Nationally, 7% of youth arrests happen at school (Justice Policy Institute, 2020), and many believe these arrests would not have happened if there were no police officers in the school. Critics of SROs think money would better be spent on counselors and other programs.

This quote from the ACLU executive summary on the white paper *Bullies in Blue*, published in April 2017 (French-Marcelin, 2017), shows the negative impacts of SROs:

> Every day in our nation's schools, children as young as five are charged with "crimes" for everyday misbehavior: throwing a paper airplane, kicking a trashcan, and wearing sagging pants. 2013-14 school year, the most recent year for which statistics are available, schools reported over 223,000 referrals to law enforcement. A 13-year-old Texas boy who attempted to pay for school lunch with a $2 bill that turned out to be fake faced prison time on charges of felony forgery. In Virginia, a middle school student was charged with assault and battery with a weapon for throwing a baby carrot at her teacher. (p. 8)

The criminalization of youth has created schools which are not places of saftey, but places where non criminal behavior can lead to arrest.

Author's note: As a former assistant principal and principal, I have worked with more than one SRO. My experiences were extremely positive. We worked as part of large administrative teams with clear communication and purpose. My SRO counterparts were able to support me as I made home visits and entered physically dangerous situations. Only in cases in which I would have called law enforcement into the school did the SROs take over; until that point discipline was handled by the school. We had a collective interest in "big picture" safety. The SROs focused on community safety, not minor infractions that could be handled by calling parents or letting administrators use the school conduct policy. We created an environment where kids could make mistakes and make reasonable repairs to their community rather than involving them in the justice system. The SROs with whom I worked engaged students at lunch, coached teams, and supported students in the community. These SROs became trusted adults who worked with me and the students to come up with solutions. The research on SROs is still inconclusive.

Alana and Tia

Alana calls the police repeatedly because her daughter Tia keeps locking herself in her room. The first few times, the police come and get the girl out of the room and tell her to behave. Alana then decides she wants her daughter charged as an incorrigible youth. On the next call to the police, she tells the police she can't handle her daughter anymore and she doesn't want her in her home. The police take Tia to the detention center pending a hearing; this would be an appropriate use of an emergency foster placement, were there an adequate number. In family court several days later, Tia claims she has been locking herself in her room because her mother has been inviting men to the house at night to prostitute herself for drugs. When the house would get busy, men would try to get into Tia's room. Tia is remanded to Department of Social Services (DSS) custody, which we see in the next story is not always a solution. Tia is not ultimately sentenced to prison time in addition to time in the detention center waiting to go to court.

Background on childhood neglect and abuse

Child abuse and neglect are underreported in the United States, with neglect being less reported than abuse since it is harder for teachers and other mandated reporters to spot. At least one in seven children has experienced child abuse or neglect in the past year in the United States. In 2020, 1,750 children died of abuse and neglect in the United States (CDC, 2022). Six broad types of neglect have been accepted as common categories, while each state has slightly different definitions of these: physical, medical, environmental, emotional, educational, and inadequate supervision (DePanfilis, 2006).

Physical neglect includes abandonment of the child, refusal to maintain custody of the child, leaving the child in the care of others, hunger, lack of clothing, and other disregard for the child's safety such as driving intoxicated with the child in the car. Medical neglect is the denial of medical care or the delay in seeking medical care, either yearly preventative care or when the child is sick. Environmental neglect is the failure to protect children from hazards in the local environment and in the home, for example, allowing children to play in the street instead of taking them to a playground. Neighborhood safety is also in this category but rarely addressed since the entire neighborhood would need intervention. Emotional neglect is the lack of affection, spousal abuse of one of the parents in the home, caregivers' drug and alcohol use, and isolation of the child. Educational neglect includes truancy and inattention to special education needs as a national standard.

The neglect seen in Tia's story above is inadequate supervision; the girl was left unsupervised in the company of inappropriate adults. This failure to protect a child is clear. It could be added that this example includes environmental neglect given the presence of inappropriate adults and illegal activity in the house.

DSS gone wrong

Seven foster children were arrested at the South Carolina DSS office. The children were charged with aggravated assault by a mob and remanded to DJJ custody. The disturbance occurred just after 8:00 p.m. The children, along with others, have been living in the DSS office. There has been an increase in the number of children sleeping on air mattresses in DSS offices across the state in the last year due to a lack of foster homes. When the end of the day comes, children need to be placed in homes or emergency placements for the night, and these have not been available. These seven children are sleeping on couches or on the floor in sleeping bags until the office opens in the morning. A staff member is left to supervise overnight but clearly could be overwhelmed by the number of displaced children they are supervising. Children removed from their homes are already coming from difficult situations, and now they are left overnight in an office.

In July 2023, foster kids spent a collective 132 nights in state offices (Thomson, 2023). Officials reported a shortage of approximately 2,000 foster homes as of August 2023. The seven teens in this story are being held at the detention center awaiting a court date in family court.

Background on foster care

Many of the children unable to be placed in a foster home are suffering from a mental health diagnosis. From April to June 2023, 79% of 109 children sleeping in DSS offices had a confirmed diagnosis (Thompson, 2023). Declining mental health continues to be an issue in foster placement, and there are not enough mental health specialists in the state. The state's lone 24-hour crisis-stabilization unit is only for adults. Parents are refusing to take their children back from custody due to the unavailability of mental health resources. This leaves children in the system bouncing from placement to placement to office air mattresses, which leads to a further decline in mental health. It is not surprising that these children become agitated while staying overnight in an office with upwards of ten other children in the same situation. South Carolina is in urgent need of foster homes.

Summary

Children enter the juvenile justice system in many ways, and several of them are consequently stuck cycling through the system. In Chapter 2, the current system is explained.

Discussion questions

1.   What have you learned about the juvenile justice system?
2.   How could these scenarios have turned out differently?
3.   Where do you stand on law enforcement in schools? Why?

Recommended assignments

1. Watch the documentary *On These Grounds* and write a reflection.

2. Interview a member of law enforcement who works with juveniles.

3. Watch a documentary such as *What Happens When a School Decides to Arrest a Juvenile?* (https://youtu.be/AVGgkwmM iac). Write a reflection.

4. Interview an SRO or a school administrator about police in schools.

Resources

Children's Trust of South Carolina. https://scchildren.org/reco gnizing-child-abuse-and-neglect/.

Feeding America. https://map.feedingamerica.org/county/ 2020/child/south-carolina.

South Carolina Association of School Resource Officers. https:// www.scasro.org/.

South Carolina Youth Advocate Program. https://scyap.com/.

South Carolina: A Hunger and Poverty Snapshot—Bread for the World. https://www.bread.org/article/south-carolina-a-hunger-and-poverty-snapshot/#:~:text=In%20South%20Carol ina%2C%20between%202019-2021%3A%201%20Food%20 insecurity,others%29%20in%20the%20state%20averaged%20 14.1%25.%20More%20items.

2

Incarceration in South Carolina: The system

Guiding Question: What is the South Carolina Department of Juvenile Justice (SCDJJ) like inside?

Learning outcomes

- Understand how the DJJ system is set up.
- Understand the varying perspectives on what the inside is like.
- Understand past allegations against SCDJJ.

Structure of SCDJJ

South Carolina DJJ's basic structure is a Cognia-accredited school district, a private accreditation certificate that is conducted in three evaluation centers, one detention center, one high school behind the fence (Birchwood), and ten camps. The school district is made up of one superintendent, four principals, one assistant principal, one special education director, and varying numbers of teachers, assistant teachers, guidance counselors, and staff. Schooling is year-round, and security permitting is offered five days a week. Camp education is contracted to private programs, but DJJ employs official teachers who set the curriculum and give grades. Teachers of record create the lessons, review work, and give grades. The school district serves approximately 500 students at any given time. In 2023, 111 students earned a GED or diploma. The first-hand accounts of the system vary from the facts and descriptions on the official website as seen in the following narrative. Students theoretically travel from short-term detention to court to evaluation center to court to Birchwood or a camp. Education takes place at evaluation centers, juvenile detention center, Birchwood, and camps.

Detention and evaluation centers

Students' educational experience begins in whatever detention center or evaluation center they are placed in. There is one for girls and two for boys. Because of the work being done at Birchwood School, behind the fence, after the 2017 federal lawsuit referenced below, many students stay in evaluation facilities far past their court date. Given the backlog since Covid-19, many students remain in the evaluation long past the 45-day maximum awaiting their court date. One staff member estimated that 45 or more students were in detention centers for more than 200 days waiting on court dates. This all means that students who are awaiting a court date on a simple truancy charge are being detained for the better part of a year in the same population as students convicted of murder. Everyone agrees that this situation is not ideal and puts low-level offenders at significant risk both physically and psychologically. Students report that those with low-level offenses are just trying to get by until court, hoping to go home on probation or to a low-security camp, while offenders with a determinate sentence know they will be transferred to adult prison on their eighteenth birthday. This dynamic creates an unsafe environment.

Once students have gone through the court system, they, in theory, are sent to Birchwood or to a camp. Currently, many stay in evaluation centers because of overcrowding, lack of security staff, and work being done at Birchwood as a result of the 2017 lawsuit. Ideally, serious offenders (murder, aggravated assault) go to Birchwood as a first step, and lower-level offenders go to a camp.

One glaring inequity in this system is gender. As of 2024, all girls referred to DJJ statewide are housed at Coastal Evaluation Center or a camp called Piedmont Wilderness Institute, a camp that has 20 beds available, even though girls make up 30% of the juvenile population referred to DJJ. Boys, who make up 70% of the referrals, have 262 alternative (camp) beds available, two evaluation facilities, and the long-term high school, Birchwood. Currently, the Coastal Evaluation Center for girls and women is being modified to better meet the needs of females since it was originally designed for men.

	% Referrals	# Alternative Beds (camps)	Percentage of Alternative Beds (Camps)	Facilities
Girls	30	20	7%	1 Evaluation Center
Boys	70	262	93%	2 Evaluation Centers
				Birchwood High School

Birchwood (high school behind the fence)

Birchwood is where the boys convicted of more serious offenders are sent. These children are housed in pods and moved to the education section of the facility as security allows. Since education is legally mandated, when students cannot move due to security reasons, teachers should go to the housing pods or isolation units to deliver daily lessons. Safety is a constant concern for teachers and impacts how and when students get their education. Each student has an individual curriculum based on their current credit level and whether they are seeking a diploma, GED, or high school credential.

Delivery of education in this locked facility is difficult due to security concerns and restrictions. Students may be placed under "no movement" with their whole pod because of fighting within the housing pod, tensions with other housing pods that preclude the groups from moving at the same time, general safety concerns, and security staffing. While these larger issues create an obstacle to educating a housing pod as a unit, individual situations also make education difficult. When a child is isolated for violent behavior, protection, or other reasons, they need a teacher to come to them. Given the staffing limitations, it is difficult to meet students' educational needs and provide legally guaranteed services when students are in isolation.

Camps

Of the ten contracted camps, there is only one for girls. Nine camps are listed on SCDJJ's official website, but ten is the number provided by DJJ (personal communication, 2024). Each camp is responsible to DJJ but is run independently by the education director or lead teacher hired by the contracted program. Camps vary in everything from dress code to basic rules governing conduct such as whether a student has to get up and go to school. Almost exclusively, the camps use teacher assistants who work in loose collaboration with the teachers of record. The teachers of record who work at Birchwood or the evaluation centers create lessons and materials and put them in an online portal for teacher assistants to access and deliver. Student work is then sent back to the teacher of record for review and grading.

News coverage of SCDJJ

While interviewing adults associated with the SCDJJ system elicits a sense of hope and forward momentum, news reports show a different story. Three recent and notable lawsuits in 2024, 2022, and 2017 paint a different picture of life inside SCDJJ (NAACP, 2022). The stories talk of neglect, constant violence, long-term isolation, lack of basic sanitary conditions, and shortage of educational services. Lawsuits are seeking clean water and food, dry beds, limitations to solitary confinement, and educational and mental health services. "South Carolina exposes the children in its juvenile justice system—most of whom are Black—to barbaric conditions", said Brenda Murphy, President of the NAACP South Carolina State Conference of Branches. "Children in custody suffer from constant violence, are isolated for weeks and months, and are denied the basic rehabilitative services they need and are entitled to. Our most vulnerable children must receive support, not punishment." (Orecchio-Egresitz, 2022)

2017 federal civil rights case— excessive force

A 2017 federal civil rights case prompted a federal investigation in which investigators spent five years investigating claims at SCDJJ. The findings were released in 2020, and on April 14, 2022, it was announced that SCDJJ agreed to fix the issues resulting from the investigation, which demonstrated a pattern of excessive force (Adcox, 2022). The investigation found that officers had broken a child's arm, bit another child after agreeing to a fight with them, and other offenses of excessive force including prolonged and punitive isolation. Between July 2018 and May 2019, there were "134 fights and 71 assaults that resulted in 99 injuries to youth in a facility with an average daily population of just over 100", according to the lawsuit, which cited a recent Justice Department report (Adcox, 2022)

The newest SCDJJ Director Eden Hendrick signed an agreement including "changes in officer training, restraining techniques, using isolation as punishment and how to respond to fights between teenagers. Other steps include overhauling the security camera system on campus" (Adcox, 2022).

Findings in the 2020 Federal Investigation Report stated that in a prison with approximately 100 juveniles, there were 99 injuries reported over 11 months. The specifics on the violence resulting in injuries included an "officer intervening in a fight by putting a teen in a chokehold" and a video showing "an officer failing to do anything while a teen was repeatedly attacked in his pod over three hours. Instead, the officer remained in his seat never calling for assistance, according to the federal report" (Adcox, 2022).

A review of dozens of other use-of-force reports wasn't possible due to the lack of video surveillance around the campus—a limitation of which agency leaders were aware. The report from the Department of Justice's Civil Rights Division ordered SCDJJ to make changes or face another lawsuit.

April 2022—civil rights lawsuit, S.C. State Conference of NAACP v. S.C. Department of Juvenile Justice

In this lawsuit, the ACLU states:

> Under the care of the S.C. Department of Juvenile Justice (DJJ), South Carolina children live in overcrowded and understaffed facilities, under threat of rampant uncontrolled violence from staff and one another, in levels of unsanitary filth that would not be acceptable for a dog kennel. (ACLU, 2022)

The original lawsuit demands that children be provided basic living needs such as clean water, healthy food, sanitary living conditions, and physical safety. The lawsuit goes on to require mental health basics such as freedom from solitary confinement, meaningful access to education, mental health resources, and accommodations for children with disabilities (ACLU, 2022).

The ACLU complaint includes individual stories from children held at DJJ as a method of describing the conditions that children are living in while incarcerated. One story documents a 14-year-old who is routinely targeted for abuse by other children and witnessed a riot where another child's jaw was broken.

Documentation of children held in isolation and not given any schoolwork shows the lack of education while incarcerated. Other children's experiences reported isolation for weeks in a wet holding cell with a broken sink and toilet and no access to a shower. One child complained of being assaulted by DJJ staff five times, including one time when he was punched so hard in the ribs that he struggled to breathe the next day (ACLU, 2022).

Throughout the lawsuit, there are references to unsanitary conditions such as sewage water in the cells, feces on the walls, and cockroaches in the food provided at the facilities. Youth-on-youth violence is constant, with staff often turning a blind eye or even instigating assaults on children. There were allegations that DJJ has resorted to 23-hour-a-day solitary confinement as a management tool to house sick kids, "protect" children from violence, or address even the most minor of infractions (NAACP, 2022).

Previous lawsuits show that DJJ was sued for violating the rights of children in 1990; lost a lawsuit in 1995 that forced it to implement policy changes; as well as paid $1.1 million in 2002 to settle claims that children as young as ten years old had been sexually assaulted in their facilities. Staff at a Columbia facility walked out in protest of unsafe conditions in June 2021. DJJ facilities have since been wracked by large-scale riots in 2022 and 2023 that left children injured and traumatized (ACLU 2024).

In addition to the unsafe and unsanitary living conditions, children are being denied their right to an education. Children have limited classes, lack access to any classes when disciplined in solitary confinement, and lose access to education when there is violence in the prison. This lack of consistent access is diffi-cult for all children, especially those with preexisting learning conditions.

January 2024—Jeffcoat civil suit

A Columbia attorney called Matthew Yelverton announced a civil rights lawsuit in early 2024 representing the mother of Easley Jeffcoat, age 16 (Hughs). According to the State, the teen was being treated at DJJ rather than incarcerated. In the absence of other immediate mental health care, DJJ was treating Jeffcoat until the family could find another residential facility.[1] The lawsuit claims negligence and civil rights violations during his time there for mental health treatment. Jeffcoat attempted suicide in the infirmary at a DJJ facility on December 6, 2023, and was taken to the hospital where he died two days later. He had been moved to the infirmary because of concerns about his mental health and suicidal thoughts. Despite the reason for him being there, his self-injurious behavior went unnoticed for an hour or longer. The ACLU of South Carolina has called the death "tragic and inex-cusable". Incidents like this one will continue happening until years of systemic failures are corrected, says Jace Woodrum, the Executive Director of the ACLU of South Carolina (Jurado, 2023). According to the ACLU, the detention center was meant to hold 72 children, yet 130 are currently awaiting trial there. The ACLU and other advocate groups such as the Children's Law Center are asking the DJJ to stop incarcerating children for status offenses of truancy, running away, and incorrigibility (personal communi-cation, June 2023).

Summary

Reconciling the picture of an accredited school district and the accusations within these lawsuits leaves one to wonder what is happening. Federal investigations have found that conditions are not acceptable, and students are not being educated as required by law. This leads citizens to question the purpose of DJJ. Is it as advertised in its mission to "impact and transform young lives, strengthen families, and support safer communities through targeted prevention and rehabilitation" or is it a place to dump kids who are causing problems? Chapter 3 looks at the adults who work with children in the justice system.

Discussion questions

1. What strikes you as the biggest disparity between the advertised DJJ system according to the website in the Introduction and reports from insiders in this chapter?
2. What questions do the lawsuits bring up for you?
3. What would you do if your family member were in the SCDJJ system?

Extension activities

1. Research what actions you could take if your family member were incarcerated in SCDJJ.
2. Review the complaints in one of the lawsuits in this chapter. What stands out for you?
3. Create your version of a mission/vision statement for the SCDJJ system. How would you restructure the department to meet this new mission/vision statement?

Note

1. *DJJ noted that they are not responsible for treating mental illness. While DJJ does care for the mental health needs of those incarcerated, they are not a treatment facility (personal communication, 2024)

Resources

America's juvenile injustice system. [Video] YouTube. Available at: https://youtu.be/8cPRB9XxOll?si=L54PN1pNHZQ5nJTg. Feb 2016.

Chaos at SC juvenile detention center. [Video] YouTube. Available at: https://www.youtube.com/watch?v=2gjjCji7nmw. April 2020

Loaded gun found inside of the SC Department of Juvenile Justice facility. [Video] YouTube. Available at: https://www.youtube.com/watch?v=8zaXRulPHnw. May 2022

Prison kids: juvenile justice in America. [Video] YouTube. Available at: https://youtu.be/5c5taQG7OX4?si=x9bFTWciY5XkjZWb. Date May 2020

3
Supporting incarcerated juveniles

Guiding Questions: Who works with children in the juvenile justice system? Why did they choose this occupation?

Learning outcomes

- Understand who works with incarcerated children.
- Understand the beliefs of those who work with the children.
- Understand the obstacles faced by these adults.

Adults working with incarcerated children

To examine who works with juveniles at DJJ, the author interviewed more than 20 adults associated with the juvenile justice system in South Carolina. Qualitative interviews were coded, and themes were identified based on the data gathered in the interviews. Participants interviewed were law officers working with juveniles, legal advocates, justice advocates, and DJJ staff or contracted staff working on the education or legal side of the DJJ system as teachers, community outreach and career development staff, and school administrators. These profession-als were primarily at the mid-to-late career stage. One participant had been in their position for more than 30 years, having never had a job outside of SCDJJ. More than one participant either had their doctorate or was in the process of earning it. Multiple partic-ipants held master's degrees in education, business, or psychol-ogy. Participants describe an overwhelming "calling" to their jobs rather than a need for a job. These are adults who have chosen "to shape the lives of children" despite difficult working condi-tions, low pay, and safety issues. Everyone interviewed described their "passion for kids" and their desire to help. The adult partic-ipants were an overwhelmingly positive, highly educated, and dedicated group of adults.

From these interviews, three themes emerged: beliefs, rela-tionship building, and obstacles. Within each theme, several subthemes were common among the participants. Within the theme of beliefs, participants noted that kids aren't bad, but fre-quently they are the victims of circumstances and are develop-mentally unable to make adult decisions. Kids deserve a second chance; staff are overwhelmingly positive about kids' abilities to turn things around and believe that success is necessary. In the theme of relationship building, participants viewed forming individual relationships with the kids they encounter as key to their ability to create success. Everyone creates relationships in their own way and with their own values. The key is having rela-tionships. Facing obstacles was theme three, and its subthemes spanned the spectrum from not being able to get students' school records to security requirements to the inability to get students through the educational system despite DJJ being its own school district.

Beliefs	Relationship Building	Obstacles
• kids aren't bad • victims of circumstance • developmental ability	• meeting kids where they are • setting limits	• records • return to community • security requirements

Beliefs

Those interviewed shared an overwhelming belief that kids are not bad. Most conversations started with statements such as …

- "These aren't bad kids."
- "These are good kids in bad situations."
- "There was no way this kid could have made it based on their home situation."
- "These kids are victims."
- "These kids are kids who were expected to handle adult problems."
- "These kids are not developmentally able to make adult choices because they are kids."

The basic story told by the adults working with incarcerated children is one of an inadequate homelife: insufficient physical resources (food, safe shelter, permanent shelter), ongoing psychological neglect or abuse (no adults regularly caring for children, multiple partial caregivers, kids caring for other kids, abuse, role confusion when boys are asked to be the "man of the house"), and inappropriate expectations (kids being asked to contribute to the family's earning rather than going to school, caring for siblings). These three factors, combined with adolescent development, led to recurring stories for many kids who are in the system.

Table: Homelife Challenges

Physical Resources	• inadequate food • lack of permanant shelter • inadequate clothing • lack of medical care
Psychological Stability	• lack of adult caregivers • multiple partial caregivers • kids caring for kids
Expectations	• kids as earners • role confusion, "man of the house" • parentifying of children

Missing tangible resources and generational poverty are the beginning of most of these stories. Generational poverty is a widely used term to describe families that live below the poverty line for two generations or more. Participants told stories about kids living in cars, on friends' porches, in parks, and couch surfing with their young siblings. This uncertain life led to stealing food or money for needs (medicine, clothes, etc.) and later arrest. Kids frequently engaged in fights to protect themselves or their siblings from predators in these constantly changing living situations. Some entered gangs to gain protection and were arrested for initiation or gang activity once they were in the lifestyle.

Many children in the juvenile system lack psychological stability. Children who come from parents who have faced or are facing their own issues are prevalently involved in psychological abuse or neglect. Some kids were left with "family" while their parents were incarcerated, and sometimes this family was a gang affiliation that indoctrinated the child further into gang life. Other kids were "sold/traded" by parents who were addicts and needed drugs but had no income. According to the South Carolina Human Trafficking Task Force, 399 children were identified as being trafficked in 2022. Still others were born to the victims of domestic abuse, rape, or incest. The children then suffered mistreatment because they reminded the parents of their physical trauma. Children coming from these environments can suffer from post-traumatic stress, psychological and emotional disorders, and attachment disorders (Muller, 2016).

Children as young as 10 to 12 years old are being asked to take on adult responsibilities, and these unrealistic expectations put kids in situations that lead to risky and dangerous behaviors. Many children were described as "having to run a household" at the age of 13 or 14. In girls' cases, this usually meant taking siblings to school, picking them up from school, foraging for food and feeding siblings, and finding a place to stay for the night. In boys' cases, this meant keeping siblings "in line", keeping the family group physically safe, and stealing money or food. This "man of the house" role led to extreme conflict for many boys when the mother took in a boyfriend who then expected the boy (previously the man of the house) to follow his rules. This cycle of going from "man of the house" to "girlfriend's kid" seemed typical for many of the boys the participants spoke about.

Adolescents are less able than adults to consider the consequences of their actions than plan for the future, control their impulses, and regulate their emotions (Denworth, 2021). Adolescents seek peer approval and respect, which makes them susceptible to peer pressure. Approximately 700,000 U.S. youth are arrested and entered into the juvenile justice system annually. Part of the underlying cause for this arrest rate is that adolescence is a time of increased risk-taking, including illegal behavior (Office of Juvenile Justice and Delinquency Prevention, 2020).

Considering the inadequate home life and the children's lack of full development, participants expressed that these kids need a second chance. There is a clear delineation in the minds of participants between second chances and letting kids "get away with their crimes". Not one participant expressed a desire to ignore the crime and some form of consequence. It was the type of consequence that was often discussed. Most participants believed that kids getting into trouble need education and mentoring rather than prison. Prevention programs were talked about frequently—programs designed to catch these kids before they made a big mistake. Kids behind the fence were likely to spend 34 to 64 months in juvenile prison, and many were sent directly to adult prison on their eighteenth birthday. This long-term incarceration is not rehabilitative; it is institutionalizing kids and making it harder for them to return to the community with any degree of success—if they ever get the opportunity. Among participants, there is a belief that with resources and education, kids can make a change for the better. Participants agreed that to change their trajectory, kids need literacy skills, career skills, mental health counseling, and in most cases a fresh start in a new community with positive adult mentors.

Relationship building

Everyone who was interviewed talked about creating relationships with kids. One administrator talked about inviting each child into their office and asking about them, their interests, and their goals. Forming relationships in a locked facility poses new challenges, though. The administrator who met with each child realized quickly that kids had no access to pens while incarcerated. In the administrator's office, kids kept touching and taking pens. The administrator had to call security before the kids went back to their pods to be sure they had not taken any pens, which are considered contraband. The importance of taking individual time with kids was a universal theme. Participants talked about getting to know individual kids and their needs. Working with families to create pathways after incarceration was also mentioned often.

One administrator talked about trying to find an aunt or uncle in another part of the state so the child could start fresh with no gang obligations. Sending the boy home to his "old" situation would be pointless. Gang members would grab him within a block of prison, and he would be back in the life, with no choices, no options. Much of the recidivism rate comes down to a family's ability to get kids out of the situation they were in before incarceration. Had the family been able to move, they often would have done it prior. Families want the best for their kids, but many times they are not able to provide it because of the circumstances they were brought into, and this speaks to intergenerational poverty.

Meeting students where they are is a common theme. Children misbehave in school when they can't perform academically, which leads to them being removed from class and beginning the school-to-prison pipeline. Frequently, students are referred to DJJ for school fights, which can lead to third-degree assault charges. Once the child is referred to DJJ, they can be expelled from school, removing the problem from the school district.

Students often arrive at DJJ "overage and under credit". This means that they have failed classes or have not been in school for an extended period. The average age of students entering DJJ is 16, approximately juniors, and the average number of credits they enter with is 5. The number of credits to graduate in South Carolina is 24, so at the end of ninth grade, students should have at least 6 credits at the average age of 14 to 15, and they should have 18 credits by the end of junior year. In addition, many students arrive with unmet federally required special education plans, both Section 504 and individualized education plan (IEP) requirements, meaning that, by federal law, they are entitled to receive educational services they have not been receiving. Students with 504s and IEPs have educational needs associated with conditions spanning from ADHD to autism. Federal law, the Individuals with Disabilities Education Act (IDEA), dictates that students receive services that most of these students referred to DJJ have not been receiving. While this is an obstacle, it is also a relationship-building moment. Rather than focusing on what has not been done and whose fault it is, interview participants see this as an opportunity to meet students where they are and build from there.

Building relationships is not just reaching kids and helping them where they are, it is reasonably setting appropriate limits. Multiple staff talked about caring enough to set limits. Kids know when you are just giving them a pass and letting them run wild because it takes too much energy to set limits and deal with the pushback. One staff member said, "Just letting kids do anything is a cop-out. They know you just don't care enough to deal with them." This approach to putting in the time to set appropriate limits speaks to relationship building because it helps kids feel cared for and important enough for an adult's time. Kids respect adults who take the time to earn respect and set limits. For example, one staff member talked about making kids earn privileges through a bracelet system at one DJJ camp. The bracelets are colored and show what level of privilege each kid has. It is hard to take away privileges because kids get angry and frustrated. But, if kids are disrespectful or do not complete a task and they lose their level of privilege, this consequence tells kids, "I care enough to set limits."

The relationship building does not end at the door; DJJ has a policy of putting eyes on kids within 48 hours. Rather than send kids out with the attitude of "We are done with you", they say, "We will see you in 48 hours—you are still ours." This message of continued care and expectations is meant to carry over to their time, post-incarceration, in the community. Unfortunately, kids are going out into unsupervised and volatile situations, and they often return to DJJ or adult prison. The recidivism rate is 34.2% according to the DJJ *Data Resource Guide* 2022–2023.

Barriers

In addition to recidivism rates, participants noted three main obstacles: lack of school records, inability to return students to community schools, and security requirements. All three challenges lead to difficulties in delivering free and appropriate education as mandated by federal law (Free and Appropriate Public Education). As an accredited school system, DJJ is held to the same standards as all other local schools despite their special circumstances.

When students enter the DJJ system, it is frequently difficult to track down their previous educational records. Many students have not been attending school with any regularity since middle school, making it difficult to locate their last school. When records are obtained, they often show low earned credit and special education plans that are incomplete or out of date. Previous schools have been unable to provide the legally mandated services necessary since students have not been in school, which immediately puts DJJ out of federal compliance. Starting out of compliance puts DJJ at a huge disadvantage in getting kids back on track. For example, if a student who was on an IEP enters DJJ, they are entitled to the services laid out in the plan. If the plan is out of date, a new IEP needs to be called and new evaluations done. Students must receive the services called for in the new IEP, such as 60 minutes a day of individual reading instruction, untimed tests, and having all tests read aloud to them. This is not unusual accommodation but requires a greater effort in a secure facility. As noted in obstacle three below, security takes priority over education.

A second obstacle faced by incarcerated kids is their inability to return to public school. In South Carolina, when kids are involved with the DJJ system, they must wait 365 days to return to public school. According to S.C. law 59-63-210, schools can expel students for any crime. An arrest alone can lead to expulsion, and if a child is incarcerated, the 365-day period for potential readmission begins upon their release. In addition to denying students access to education, this sends the message that they are not welcome back in the community. One example of this was a student who, after two and a half years of incarceration, had earned all but 12 credits toward a high school diploma. He was not allowed back in his home public school for one calendar year (365 days). His crime was committed in the community, not in the school; he had no recorded behavior issues in school; and he had received straight As until being incarcerated. The only way to get the boy a diploma was for DJJ to create an online program for him so he could earn his last credits. He completed his degree from a neighboring state in the custody of his grandmother. He started a four-year college as a residential student within months of earning his diploma, and he is doing well. (This student will remain anonymous.)

Security requirements are perhaps the biggest set of obstacles faced by the DJJ educational staff. Despite the legal obligation to provide education and meet special education law service requirements, security takes precedence at a secure facility. The movement of kids determines how education is delivered. If there is tension between two pods, kids in those pods cannot go to the school section of the building together. Thus, their time in school may be cut in half, with each pod taking half of the day. Since pods can't pass in the building, there is lost time between securing groups.

If there are not enough security officers to move kids who are considered dangerous, then the educators need to go to the kids' pod to teach. Teaching in the pod does not offer the same security for staff that teaching in the school section does. Teaching in the pod is equivalent to teaching a student in their own home, in that the students know the surroundings and could have hidden weapons. The climate while teaching in the pod is also different since you are in the kids'"homes" rather than the teacher's classroom. The physical design of the pod also eliminates safety measures for staff. The tables are bolted in the middle of the common room, so teachers cannot have their backs to the wall and cannot arrange furniture to ensure that kids are looking at the walls so they cannot communicate with each other. The teacher cannot easily see what each student is doing. In addition, the pod common areas accommodate more students than the smaller classrooms do, making it harder to provide physical safety to educators. In the school setting, there are fewer students, smaller spaces that can be locked down, more adults, and, in some cases, part of a rapid response team is stationed nearby.

Another challenge for education staff is teaching students in isolation. When a student is put into isolation for behavioral issues, they are still legally entitled to receive education services. In the case of a student with an IEP that says they need 60 minutes of direct instruction in reading, a teacher must go to isolation and provide 60 minutes of direct instruction; work cannot just be sent to the student in isolation. Sending work to a student in isolation creates security issues since students are not allowed to have basic school items without direct supervision. This tension between security and education creates a complicated system. The system itself becomes an obstacle to educating children who, for the most part, entered the system already behind and disengaged.

Despite the obstacles, the DJJ school superintendent works from a belief that "Success is the only option." Failing will only send kids back to the community even more unprepared to succeed.

To incarcerate and thereby institutionalize a child and then send them back to the place where they already failed, with no new skills, is dooming them to increasingly worse outcomes. The only way to change the cycle of incarceration is to educate children.

Summary

Those who choose to work with incarcerated youth talk about their basic beliefs in children's underlying good qualities, building strong relationships with youth, and the obstacles they face when working within the system. These educators recognize that many of these children come from an inadequate home life. Children are coming into the system lacking physical resources, psychological stability, and clear expectations. Chapter 4 will examine what it is like to be incarcerated.

Discussion questions

1. As a nation, we incarcerate more youth than any other developed country. Why?
2. Why are relationships the common denominator in creating success within the system?
3. How do we keep youth from being incarcerated?

Extension activities

1. Research the school-to-prison pipeline and write an op-ed for a local paper.
2. Watch the video on mass incarceration and reflect on your reaction to the statistics.
3. Research resources for teens in your state. Write an article or flier to help teens in need find the right resources.

Resources

School to prison pipeline. [Video] YouTube. Available at: https://www.youtube.com/watch?v=HoKkasEyDOl. Jan 2016.

Mass incarceration. [Video] YouTube. Available at: https://www.youtube.com/watch?v=u51_pzax4M0. Oct 2016.

Palmetto Place: children & youth services. Available at: https://www.palmettoplace.org/.

4
Life inside

Guiding Question: What is it like to be inside the juvenile detention system?

Learning outcomes

- Understand what kids experience.
- Understand what kids are telling adults.

Talking directly to incarcerated children is difficult and could feel coercive to children. To "hear" what kids are thinking and feeling, this chapter relies on adult participants conveying what they have heard or seen from kids, interviews from post-incarcerated youth, and surveys given during E.A.R.N. programming. E.A.R.N. the Right is a nonprofit group that teaches communication skills to students through a six-hour program offered at some DJJ camps and evaluation centers. The adults are able to relay what is happening with children and what children are talking about without upsetting the children in custody. Children's voice is heard through the adults they trust enough to talk to.

Stories from adult advocates

First, it is important to hear kids' stories from the adults who advocate for them. The interviews from the previous chapter were coded to separate themes from the youth stories that participants had heard. The interviews revealed three themes: fear, uncertainty, and hope for the future.

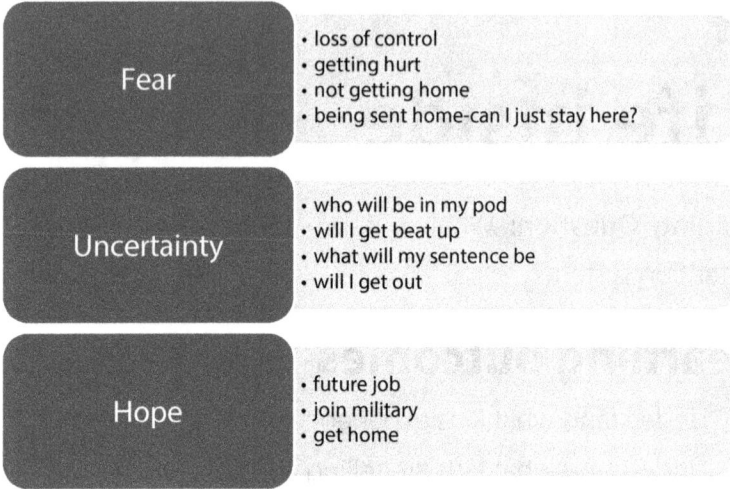

Fear	• loss of control • getting hurt • not getting home • being sent home-can I just stay here?
Uncertainty	• who will be in my pod • will I get beat up • what will my sentence be • will I get out
Hope	• future job • join military • get home

Fear

When a youth enters the system, they start in a state of fear, especially if it is their first time in the system. Children lose all control of their daily lives when incarcerated, and this is worsened by their age since they are unable to make decisions on their own behalf medically, legally, and in all other aspects. These children have no control over where they go, even post-incarceration, since they are still juveniles. Either the state or their parent or guardian will make decisions.

Fear about post-incarceration placement is significant since it is out of the decision-making scope of juveniles. Many children are desperate to get out of the physical system and "go home". They crave their family and their home. They talk about home-cooked meals, their bed, sleeping safely, and showering at home. Other less-fortunate juveniles are worried about being sent home. The fear they experience inside is more predictable than the fear they face at home. Some youth talk about the inside as a place where "at least" they are getting fed and know where they will wake up in the morning.

Given the volatility of an uncertain future and the lack of children's developmental growth, it is no surprise that juvenile detention facilities are more volatile than adult prisons. Many of the interviewed adults discussed the volatility of juveniles based on age, brain development, future uncertainty, and general inexperience with the system. Some of the juveniles know they have a determinate sentence and therefore will move to adult prison on their eighteenth birthday, so they have no incentive to behave while in juvenile facilities. This lack of incentive makes the older, more serious offenders more violent and more likely to physically harm other inmates. Physical safety is a huge concern for incarcerated youth. Children tell staff and teachers that they are concerned about getting hurt in the housing pods where there is less supervision.

Uncertainty

Uncertainty is linked to the fear; the two are cyclical. The uncertainty of not knowing who will be in the housing pod leads to fear. The housing pod is a pivotal group of peers and affects day-to-day living and safety, when violent or combative children enter a housing pod it creates an increased potential injury to the others. Safety is a major part of the uncertainty.

Youth also worry about their future. Those who have not yet been sentenced worry about what the judge will decide. Where will I be sent? How long will I be there? Where will I go next? When will I get out? The uncertainty is illustrated in the following story. A boy, John (pseudonym), was out for a night with friends. His friends decided to find a rival group's party and try to get in. When they got to the party, they were not let in, and they left after a fistfight. One of the friends went and got guns from an older sibling. John and his friends carried out a drive-by shooting of the party, injuring party guests. One guest ended up in a long-term coma. John was arrested for being part of a drive-by shooting resulting in injuries. The incident was considered attempted murder. He was convicted and sent to Birchwood for a period. After doing well at Birchwood, John was transitioned to a camp setting as a step in the transition back into the community. One day the deputies arrived at camp and rearrested him. The victim of the shooting, who had been in a coma, died. John's charge was now murder, and, given his current age, he awaited a new sentence among the adult population.

Hope

In juxtaposition to the fear and uncertainty, there is also hope among the incarcerated youth. They hope for the time they will get out. Many aspire to join the military or get a professional license such as a CDL or electrician certification. Students who have earned a GED or diploma while incarcerated are thinking about college or a trade. For the students who can keep hope for the future, the adult advocates in their lives hope for their success. Success is universal: not returning to the system.

Kid's voices

When students engage in E.A.R.N. the Right, they fill out surveys about their desire to enter the program and how it will help them.

The students who can engage in the program are a skewed sample of the entire population within DJJ. These are students who are at a camp or an evaluation center, not at Birchwood (behind the fence). Students who are allowed to attend the program are not disruptive, and they follow the facility rules. While in the program, students are supervised by facility staff.

Students seem to be struggling to be heard and be seen for who they are and who they want to be. Three of the most powerful categories of survey responses are around the idea of "I am", "I need", and "I want to be".

I am...	I need...	Obstacles
• smart	• people to know I'm not my past	• anger
• caring		• self - sabotage
• kind	• to be understood	• keeping my mouth shut
• strong	• a chance	• White people language
• hard working	• a job	• rejection
• determined	• my freedom	• my past
• responsible	• help	• court
• good	• self confidence	• parole
• cool	• to know which words to use	• being locked up
• not a bad person	• anything - I need a lot	• my attitude
• a changed person	• a release date	• being broke
• not the reason I am here	• a safe home	• I'm shy
• powerful	• a positive peer group	• I won't change
• that nigga	• an opportunity	

Students define themselves as "good", and there is an overwhelming feeling that they need to show people they are good. This need to prove themselves seems to weigh heavily on how they want to be seen. They often use value-laden words like "strong, kind, powerful, good" to describe what they are trying to be, even though these are not concrete goals. Most students are trying to distance themselves from their mistakes.

Their needs range from general freedom to specifics like a safe home. Students want a chance to change and to improve their lives. Students see themselves as part of their obstacle to success, citing their anger, shyness, past, and inability to change. It is interesting to note that about half of the obstacles cited are self-characteristics, even though many are working to change these qualities. There is a palpable fear that they will not be able to improve.

Parts of the surveys also ask about success: what it is, what it looks like, and how to get it. Students report that…

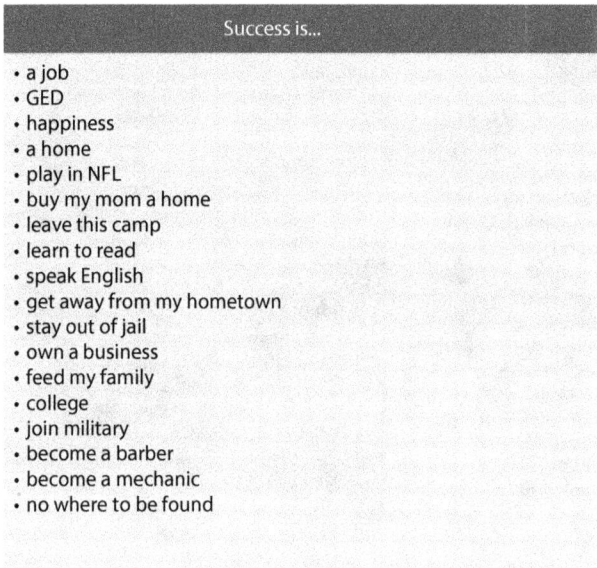

Success is...
• a job
• GED
• happiness
• a home
• play in NFL
• buy my mom a home
• leave this camp
• learn to read
• speak English
• get away from my hometown
• stay out of jail
• own a business
• feed my family
• college
• join military
• become a barber
• become a mechanic
• no where to be found

Success looks different for everyone, and some don't see it in their future.

Summary

Those who choose to work with incarcerated youth talk about their basic beliefs in children's goodness, building strong relationships with youth, and the obstacles they face when working within the system. They recognize that many children come from inadequate home environments. Children are coming into the system lacking physical recourses, psychological stability, and without clear expectations. Chapter 5 will focus on recommendations for improving outcomes for incarcerated children.

Discussion questions

1. What are your reactions to what youth are saying?
2. How do you define success?
3. How do programs like E.A.R.N. the Right impact incarcerated children?
4. What does the recidivism rate say to you?

Extension activities

1. Watch the video "The Making of a Juvenile Delinquent" (hhttps://youtu.be/JWrJTt1I2WQ?si=Xfn2IdD4ryi81R1d). May 2023. or a similar story about the road to detention. How can we change the future of kids and keep them out of the system?
2. Research the recidivism rate in your state. What efforts are being made to reduce it?
3. Watch the video "Incarcerated Children Are Still Children" (https://youtu.be/jjlEpkQYqSw?si=0A03QrKk1Re9jfvb). Review the section on the cost of incarcerating a child for a year versus the cost of a Harvard education (starting at minute 8:00). Based on the statistic quoted that one year in juvenile detention is more expensive than a prestigious four-year degree, including room and board, what would you recommend?

Resources

An insider's plan for rehabilitating the juvenile justice system. [Video] YouTube. Available at: https://youtu.be/TOxpjjzP6lM?si=DzHp4_r2ihkAVmh8.

E.A.R.N. the Right, Inc. https://www.earntheright.org/.

Incarcerated children are still children. [Video] YouTube. Available at: https://youtu.be/jjlEpkQYqSw?si=Ph0Lyzl8RUwucq7M.

Inside juvenile detention (Virginia Prison). [Video] YouTube. Available at: https://youtu.be/cLjXBwx7ja8?si=H6qnEp_Rn8fd3_HG.

Kids in juvenile prison—full documentary: Abel, Andrew and Bobby behind bars. [Video] YouTube. Available at: https://youtu.be/cLjXBwx7ja8?si=H6qnEp_Rn8fd3_HG.

The juvenile justice system is broken. Here is what actually works. [Video] YouTube. Available at: https://youtu.be/q1fsysGy_hM?si=c3Y7rS2hNU6qhDGX.

The making of a juvenile delinquent. [Video] YouTube. Available at: https://youtu.be/JWrJTt1I2WQ?si=7MQt0bb-_YNmQpqY.

When a 16-year-old is locked up in a supermax prison | Stickup kid | FRONTLINE (Juveniles in adult prison/From runaway to supermax). [Video] YouTube. Available at: https://youtu.be/z0xmAA6lPhU?si=dENve0JG4qm3mWmZ.

5
Recommendations for change

Guiding Questions: What needs to be done? What are the implications?

Learning outcomes

- Understand how DJJ can improve.
- Understand how the community can improve outcomes of previously incarcerated.

Moving forward, there are many opportunities to improve the juvenile justice system. Changes start with law and policy, which decide who is sentenced to incarceration. Then, during incarceration, there is an opportunity to provide intentional staff who are confident in their ability to connect with children for rehabilitation purposes. Education while incarcerated can create the foundation for post-incarceration success, as can a successful post-incarceration plan. And finally, there is a significant opportunity for changing the culture of the entire system from schools to courtrooms to prisons and communities.

Law/policy

The most obvious first step in improving the juvenile justice system is to prohibit minors from being incarcerated for misdemeanors, most notably the three status offenses discussed earlier: truancy, running away, and incorrigibility. Incarcerating children for misdemeanors can lead to increased criminalization (Gupta-Kagan et al., 2017). Prohibiting runaways from being incarcerated will highlight the current practice of incarcerating girls (there are a few boys, but this happens primarily to girls) who have been sex-trafficked. This will create the need for alternative programming for these girls since incarceration is currently being used as a placement.

Changing the policy around how children move through the system creates an opportunity as well. By decentralizing juvenile facilities, DJJ can expose children to fewer other inmates and locate them closer to family.

Recommendation: Prohibit incarceration for status offenses and misdemeanors. Create smaller, more supportive environments for juveniles, which would include increasing the number of alternative placements.

Education

Students historically enter the juvenile justice system "overage and under credit", and since education is a cornerstone of success, how do students get an intensive education while in the system and create a path back to education post-incarceration? The path back to education would require a law/policy change around the exclusion from community schools for 365 days post-involvement with the system. To provide an intense and appropriate education for children, we need qualified teachers who have been trained in trauma-informed practices. Having a few teachers centrally create lessons and "send them out" to the teacher assistants does not give students the best chance for success.

Recommendation: Increase the number of trauma-informed teaching staff and prioritize education.

Recruitment and retention of staff

Recruiting and retaining staff for juvenile corrections is difficult across the nation. Tipton (2002) notes that there was a lack of African American staff in SCDJJ even though African Americans comprise the majority of the inmates (p. 92). Female officers report feeling less safe than male officers in SCDJJ according to the Tipton study. Since Director Hendrick has stepped into the SCDJJ system, pay for staff has increased, and the staffing shortages have begun to lessen.

Interviews with current staff point to two areas for improvement in retention of current staff: increase the number of Black male role models, provide job security, and create a safer working environment.

Black male teachers and role models

Given that the population of juvenile incarceration in South Carolina is disproportionally Black males, it is incumbent on the system to provide Black male role models and teachers for these students. Multiple staff members noted the lack of role models to whom students can relate.

> Black boys cannot be what they cannot see. Black men speak the same language and share similar experiences and struggles as those Black boys are going to go through. Black male educators hold Black male students to higher standards and give them the inspiration, aspiration, and accountability they need. (Rodgers and Rodgers, 2023, p. 6)

Allowing students to see a role model who looks like them is critical in helping them envision success. Ray discusses four key reasons that Black male mentors are essential: they are culturally responsive, they reinforce positive racial identity, they have critical consciousness, and they address opportunity gaps (Ray, n.d.).

Job security and a safer working environment

Multiple interviewees talked about the fear of getting fired for protecting themselves or getting hurt. Other than the obvious concern about physical harm to self, staff are worried about workers' compensation and what they would do if they were injured and could not work. In the minds of some staff, the worst-case scenario would be that they would heal physically but could not go back inside to work. No one wanted to elaborate on specifics, so a story from the news demonstrates their concerns. In October 2022, carpentry teacher Wes Laws was attacked in his classroom. It was reported that a staffing shortage, specifically a 38.7% vacancy rate at the Broad River Road facility (Birchwood), led to this incident (Joseph, 2023). A juvenile attacked the teacher with tools taken from the carpentry room. Then multiple students took tools and began to riot on campus, destroying property and threatening students and staff. Before the incident, Laws had written an email to Director Hendrick:

> The stress for all of us is becoming unbearable and I am asking for help to stop this madness before someone is killed or seriously injured. From talking with others, I am not the only person that feels this way. I have had conversations with my fellow teachers, other staff members, JCOs, the contracted security, and our students. We are all afraid that someone is going to be killed, injured or they are afraid for their safety. Our students are afraid for their lives and safety. They have confided in me that the others are out of control. Our students have told me that the reason is that there are no consequences or repercussions for their actions. (Joseph, 2023)

Recommendation: Recruit Black male role models as teaching and other educational staff. Create a safe teaching environment with added security measures.

Post-incarceration

When students are released from incarceration, they are released to an adult as they are juveniles. Some return to their parents at home, while others go to foster homes or group homes. Students are not allowed to attend public schools for 365 days post-incarceration, so what do they do? They can attend online classes, they can move to a relative's house in another state, they can finish a GED, or they can get a job. What are their job prospects? As a community, are we bringing these students back to a community that provides opportunities, or are communities saying, "You are not welcome"?

Recommendation: For children to be successful, they need to leave incarceration and move to an environment where success has been set up for them. They need to go to a safe home with adequate food and supervision. They need a purpose: either work or education. And they need to be surrounded by positive adults and mentors.

Culture

All humans need to be treated with dignity and respect; children need more caring since they are still children. Punishing children does not teach them how to behave; it only teaches them what not to do. Flipping an institutional culture from one of punitive reactions to one where children are actively put in situations for success will take time and intentionality. As an interview participant said, "There is no other option." Without cultural mechanisms supporting their success, these children are destined to a life of incarceration.

Reyes, Radina and Aronson (2018) talk about radical love in teaching. Their book, "Teaching Against the Grain", espouses three keys to teaching vulnerability: collective support, healing, and critique. hooks wrote prolifically about the concept of transformation through radical love in social justice and education. Olave, Tolbert and Frausto Aceves (2023) discuss radical love as growing from a collective, righteous anger at injustice They also echo Reyes, Radina and Aronson (2018) in positioning radical love as a theory of caring, community, and mutual respect. "In thinking of the culture around troubled children, we need to embrace them as they are and help them move toward success." Radical love in juvenile detention includes compassion and transformation. This is closely related to the vision of SCDJJ.

Recommendation: Work toward a culture of radical love for the children in the juvenile system. Embrace the opportunity to create success in children.

Summary

There are many opportunities to improve the SCDJJ. These solutions require funding and reframing of how children are treated when they make mistakes. There is room for a healthy balance of accountability and rehabilitation.

Discussion questions

1.   What do you think should be the first improvement to the justice system?

2.   What one change do you think would be most impactful on changing recidivism rates?

3.   What do you think about the theory of radical love in juvenile justice?

Extension activities

1.   Find an article by bell hooks or Paulo Freire about radical love and activism. How does this approach change the way we interact with incarcerated children?

2.   Read the Juvenile Justice Report cited in the References section and write your own white paper on juvenile justice reform.

3.   Examine juvenile justice reform elsewhere; what are they doing well? What practices could be brought to South Carolina?

Resources

Radical love: How radical love transformed a school. [Video] YouTube. Available at: https://www.youtube.com/watch?v=dIYz pNAOpj8.

References

ACLU South Carolina. (2022, April 27). *Children in custody at South Carolina juvenile justice centers held in nightmarish conditions, new lawsuit alleges.* [Online] Available at: https://www.aclusc.org/en/press-releases/sc-djj-case-apr-2022 [Accessed January 2, 2023].

ACLU South Carolina. *SC NAACP v. SC Department of Juvenile Justice.* [Online] Available at: https://www.aclusc.org/en/cases/sc-naacp-v-sc-department-juvenile-justice [Accessed January 3, 2023].

Adcox, S. (2022, April 14). SC DJJ enters settlement with federal agency over civil rights violations. [Online] *The Post and Courier.* Available at: https://www.postandcourier.com/columbia/sc-djj-enters-settlement-with-federal-agency-over-civil-rights-violations/article_118bb31a-bbff-11ec-ad30-e317025971b6.html [Accessed January 4, 2023].

Aizer, A. and Doyle, J. J., Jr. (2015). Juvenile Incarceration, Human Capital, and Future Crime: Evidence from Randomly Assigned Judges. *The Quarterly Journal of Economics*, 130(2), pp. 759–803. Available at: http://doi.org/10.1093/qje/qjv003 [Accessed January 4, 2023].

Altschuler, D. M. and Brash, R. (2004). Adolescent and Teenage Offenders Confronting the Challenges and Opportunities of Reentry. *Youth Violence and Juvenile Justice*, 2(1), pp. 72–87. Available at: https://doi.org/10.1177/1541204003260048.

American Civil Liberties Union. (2019, March 4). *Cops and no counselors.* [Online] Available at: https://www.aclu.org/publications/cops-and-no-counselors.

Castle, J. (2019, July 2). What to feed your child to support healthy brain development. [Online] *U.S. News & World Report.*

Available at: https://health.usnews.com/wellness/for-parents/articles/nutrition-tips-to-support-healthy-brain-development-throughout-childhood#:~:text=Many%20nutrients%20are%20needed%20for%20normal%2C%20healthy%20brain,impact%20of%20a%20nutrient%20deficiency%20than%20older%20brains.

Cavanagh, C. (2022). Healthy Adolescent Development and the Juvenile Justice System: Challenges and Solutions. *Child Development Perspectives,* 16(3), pp. 141–147. Available at: https://srcd.onlinelibrary.wiley.com/doi/full/10.1111/cdep.12461#cdep12461-bib-0008.

Centers for Disease Control and Prevention (CDC). (2022). *Fast Facts: Preventing Child Abuse & Neglect.* Atlanta, GA: National Center for Injury Prevention and Control, Division of Violence Prevention.

Cleary, T. (2021, April 8). Niya Kenny: 5 fast facts you need to know. [Online] Heavy.com. Available at: https://heavy.com/news/2015/10/niya-kenny-assault-at-spring-valley-high-disturbing-school-south-carolina-student-video-arrested-standing-up-speaking-recording-charged-interview-mother/.

Coleman-Jensen, A., Rabbitt, M. P., Gregory, C. A. and Singh, A. (2018, May 17). *Household Food Security in the United States in 2017.* [ebook] Washington, DC: U.S. Department of Agriculture, Economic Research Service. Available at: https://www.ers.usda.gov/webdocs/publications/90023/err-256.pdf [Accessed August 6, 2024].

Cusick, S. E. and Georgieff, M. K. (2016). The Role of Nutrition in Brain Development: The Golden Opportunity of the "First 1000 Days". *The Journal of Pediatrics,* 175, pp. 16–21.

Denworth, L. (2021, May 1). Adolescent brains are wired to want status and respect: that's an opportunity for teachers and parents. [Online] *Scientific American.* Available at: https://www.scientificamerican.com/article/adolescent-brains-are-wired-to-want-status-and-respect-thats-an-opportunity-for-teachers-and-parents/ [Accessed August 6, 2024].

DePanfilis, D. (2006). *Child Neglect: A Guide for Prevention, Assessment, and Intervention*. Washington, DC: U.S. Department of Health and Human Services.

Federal Interagency Reentry Council. (2012). *Reentry Myth Buster*. New York: National Reentry Resource Center. Available at: https://juvenilecouncil.ojp.gov/sites/g/files/xyckuh301/files/media/document/reentry_council_mythbuster_it_juveniles.pdf [Accessed August 6, 2024].

French-Marcelin, M. (2017). Bullies in blue. [Online] ACLU. Available at: https://www.aclu.org/issues/juvenile-justice/school-prison-pipeline/bullies-blue [Accessed August 6, 2024].

Gupta-Kagan, J., McCormick, N., Meriwether, R. and Glenn, J. (2017, April). In Their Own Words: One Child's Tour Through DJJ. In: *Effective Solutions to South Carolina's Juvenile Justice Crisis*. South Carolina: Protection & Advocacy for People with Disability and Nelson Mullins Riley & Scarborough LLP. Available at: https://pandasc.org/wp-content/uploads/2017/04/Juvenile-Justice-Report.pdf [Accessed August 6, 2024].

Hernandez, A. (2023, December 17). Lower recidivism rates reported in several states in 2023. [Online] Stateline.org. Available at: https://www.corrections1.com/re-entry-and-recidivism/lower-recidivism-rates-reported-in-several-states-in-2023.

Hughes, M. (2023, December 28). Family of teen who died after suicide attempt at SC DJJ plans to file civil rights lawsuit. [Online] The State. https://www.aol.com/family-teen-died-suicide-attempt-172608213.html#:~:text=The%20family%E2%80%99s%20lawsuit%20will%20allege%20that%20DJJ%20was,the%20first%20of%20the%20year%20for%20administrative%20reasons [Accessed August 6, 2024].

Human Impact Partners (2017, February). *Juvenile injustice: charging youth as adults is ineffective, biased, and harmful*. [Online] Available at: https://humanimpact.org/hipprojects/juvenile-injustice-charging-youth-as-adults-is-ineffective-biased-and-harmful/ [Accessed August 6, 2024].

Joseph, C. (2023, February 16). DJJ security left a teacher alone with juveniles and tools despite pleas, attack followed. [Online] WIS News 10. Available at: https://www.wistv.com/2023/02/16/djj-security-left-teacher-alone-with-juveniles-tools-despite-pleas-attack-followed/ [Accessed August 6, 2024].

Jurado, A. (2023, December 8). ACLU demands action following attempted suicide, death of teen at DJJ facility. [Online] The State. https://news.yahoo.com/aclu-demands-action-following-attempted-172746689.html [Accessed August 6, 2024].

Muller, R. (2016, January 22). Children born of rape face a painful legacy. Clinical Practice, Research, Therapy. [Blog] The Trauma and Mental Health Report. Available at: https://trauma.blog.yorku.ca/2016/01/children-born-of-rape-face-a-painful-legacy/ [Accessed August 6, 2024].

NAACP. (2022, April 27). *New: NAACP files lawsuit in South Carolina.* [Online] https://naacp.org/articles/new-naacp-files-lawsuit-south-carolina [Accessed January 4, 2023].

Office of Juvenile Justice and Delinquency Prevention, Department of Justice. (2020). *2019 Annual Report.* Washington, DC: Office of Juvenile Justice and Delinquency Prevention.

Orecchio-Egresitz, H. (2022, May 3). Children detained in South Carolina live with feces on floors, mold on walls, and roaches in their food, suit says. [Online] Business Insider. Available at: https://www.businessinsider.com/south-carolina-rights-groups-sue-over-abuse-of-juvenile-detainees-2022-4 [Accessed August 6, 2024].

Popkin, S., Scott, M. M. and Galvez, M. M. (2016, September 12). Impossible choices: teens and food insecurity in America. [Online] Urban Institute. Available at: https://policycommons.net/artifacts/631898/impossible-choices/1613247/. CID: 20.500.12592/5mn4n6 [Accessed September 13, 2023].

RAND. (2014). *2014 RAND Annual Report.* Santa Monica, CA: RAND Corporation. Available at: https://www.rand.org/pubs/corporate_pubs/CP1-2014.html [Accessed August 6, 2024].

Ray, A. (n.d.). Black male mentors: top 4 reasons why they are essential. [Online] The Blue Heart Foundation. Available at: https://theblueheartfoundation.org/black-male-mentors-top-4-reasons-why-they-are-essential/.

Reyes, G., Radina, R. and Aronson, B. A. (2018). Teaching against the grain as an act of love: disrupting white Eurocentric masculinist frameworks within teacher education. *The Urban Review*, 50, pp. 818–835. Available at: https://doi.org/10.1007/s11256-018-0474-9.

Rodgers, B. J., Jr. and Rodgers, D. (2023). The Need for Black Male Mentors. *Kappan*, 104(7), pp. 25–29. Available at: https://kappanonline.org/the-need-for-black-male-mentors-rodgers/.

Salmassi, M. (2012). Survey finds 17% of high school students abuse substances during school day. [Online] Partnership to End Addiction. Available at: https://drugfree.org/drug-and-alcohol-news/survey-finds-17-of-high-school-students-abuse-substances-during-school-day/ [Accessed August 6, 2024].

Simonpillai, R. (2021, September 21). On these grounds: a shocking film about police brutality within US schools. [Online] The Guardian. Available at: https://www.theguardian.com/film/2021/sep/21/on-these-grounds-documentary-police-brutality-us-schools.

Snyder, H. N. and Sickmund, M. (2006). *Juvenile Offenders and Victims: 2006 National Report*. Washington, DC: U.S. Department of Justice, Office of Justice Programs, Office of Juvenile Justice and Delinquency Prevention.

South Carolina Department of Juvenile Justice. (2021). *Data Resource Guide 2020-2021*. [Online] Available at: https://djj.sc.gov/sites/djj/files/Documents/PbS%20PDFs/Resource%20Guide%20FY%202020-2021%20FINAL.pdf.

The Sentencing Project. (2023, May 16). *Policy brief: Youth justice by the numbers*. [Online] Available at: https://www.sentencingproject.org/policy-brief/youth-justice-by-the-numbers/.

Thompson, A. (2023, August 13). SC children spent hundreds of nights in state offices in overloaded foster care system. [Online] Post and Courier. Available at: https://www.postandcourier.com/ politics/sc-children-spent-hundreds-of-nights-in-state-offices-in-overloaded-foster-care-system/article_2da539fe-3615-11ee-a01a-ab96df14a349.html.

Tipton, J. A. (2002). Attitudes and Perceptions of South Carolina's Juvenile Correctional Officers, Insight into the Turnover Epidemic. *Journal of Crime and Justice,* 25(1), pp. 81–98. Available at: https:// doi.org/10.1080/0735648X.2002.9721146.

Torres Olave, B., Tolbert, S. and Frausto Aceves, A. (2023). Reflecting on Freire: A Praxis of Radical Love and Critical Hope for Science Education. *Cultural Studies of Science Education 18,* pp. 1–20. Available at: https://doi.org/10.1007/s11422-023-10168-1.

USDA. (2023). *Definitions of food security.* [Online] Available at: https://www.ers.usda.gov/topics/food-nutrition-assistance/ food-security-in-the-u-s/definitions-of-food-security/#:~:text= Food%20insecurity%E2%80%94the%20condition%20asses sed,may%20result%20from%20food%20insecurity.

Widra, E. and Herring, T. (2021). States of incarceration. [Online] Prison Policy Initiative. Available at: https://www.prisonpolicy. org/global/2021.html

Wisevoter. (2021) *Recidivism rate by state.* [Online] Available at: https://wisevoter.com/state-rankings/recidivism-rates-by-state/.

Index